Murray has gifted us a remarkable and honest story of a country boy from Surat who grew to exemplify the values of integrity, loyalty, courage, compassion and hard work. His success as a coach flows from his innate understanding that the development of sporting talent (or any talent for that matter) is best realised if you nurture and respect the person before the talent. It is not surprising Murray is approaching his next journey through Parkinson's with the same courage and resilience he has always embraced.

Katrina Robertson – World Powerlifting Champion and Psychologist

When Murray and I first brainstormed the ideas for this book, I had no idea of the drama, devastation and disappointments he has endured during his life. The story that unfolded needs to be told. Murray not only wanted to clear the air about his controversial period as a professional Rugby League coach but also to highlight his extraordinary life as a mental health advocate, business executive, politician and – above all else – a family man.

Murray Clifford – Journalist, Communications/ Photography Specialist

In *On Shaky Ground*, Murray takes us on a journey through the highs and lows of his time as an NRL coach. Murray provides an insight into the sacrifices made by rugby league players and coaches in pursuit of sporting and financial success. Murray's vision to recognise the welfare of players and the mental health challenges they face makes it a must-read for coaches and all involved in sport.

Adair Donaldson – Director, Donaldson Law

Murray's story is engaging and captivating as well as heartbreaking. He has had so many high points in his life but beautifully reveals his struggles as well in this warts and all story. Murray was a kid from country Queensland who leaves a legacy across Rugby League that will be spoken about long after he is gone. Truly inspirational.

David Solomona – QLD Wellbeing and Education Programs Manager, Rugby League Central QLD

On Shaky Ground

To my parents, Jack and Noela, for showing me the importance of good parenting and hard work. To my children, Yana and Jarrod, for their strong values. And to my wife, Pam, for raising them, and supporting and loving me over the past 40 years.

This memoir is dedicated to the five of you.

On Shaky Ground

The Murray Hurst story

Murray Hurst

On Shaky Ground: The Murray Hurst story

Author – Murray Hurst

© Murray Hurst 2021

E: hurstmurray@yahoo.com
www.murrayhurst.com

This book is sold with the understanding that the author is not offering specific personal advice to the reader. The author disclaims any responsibility for liability, loss or risk, personal or otherwise, which eventuates from using or applying any of the contents of this book.

All rights reserved. No part of this publication may not be reproduced in whole or part, stored, posted on the internet, or transmitted in any form or by any means, electronic, mechanical, photocopying, recording, or other, without permission from the author of this book.

Editing, design and publishing support by
www.AuthorSupportServices.com

ISBN: 978-1-922375-12-4

 A catalogue record for this book is available from the National Library of Australia

Acknowledgements

Thank you to my parents: although they passed away ten years apart, it is only in the time since that I realised I never asked them enough questions regarding their lives and upbringing. This prompted me to write this book for my own family. I also believe there's no better way to grow up than on the land, so thanks, Mum and Dad.

To Pam: I'm so blessed to have you as my wife forever. And to our children, Yana and Jarrod, who I love so much. I'm grateful for all your support throughout writing this memoir.

To Donella, Peta, Terry and Hilton: being your brother is a blessing, as there's never been a cross word between us. Thank you, all.

To Wayne Bennett: having you write the foreword for my memoir is a privilege. You've been a confidant to many people over many years in many walks of life, not just Rugby League. Our talks during our 30 years of friendship have always focused on life. I'm very grateful.

To Paul Bowman: you're not only one of the most honest, humble people I know but also an excellent footballer and all-round sportsman. Though you don't often voice your opinions, they always have a theme of common sense. Thank you for your contribution to this book.

To all the people I've worked with and coached over my life: I thank you very much. You've all helped me to learn about people and taught me the importance of listening, no matter who the person or what the topic is.

To David Solomona: I appreciate you and your loyalty. We worked together in wellbeing and education for a long time. You exemplify the dedicated husband and father who values your family and their health more than your own.

To Murray Clifford: you not only suggested that I write a book but also helped me write it. I don't think this would all have unfolded without your journalism background and your persistence. Thank you very much too.

Foreword

Inviting Murray Hurst to coach Brisbane Brothers Rugby League Club and take on a support role with the Broncos at the end of the 1990 Rugby League season was an easy call to make. Those who knew Murray all spoke of his honesty and integrity. They were right – he was genuine with all that he spoke of. He was also very surprised to be offered the role, and his major concern was relocating his family. He was a manager at Trans Australia Airlines in Mackay at the time, so he had a lot to consider.

I noted how Murray had brought the teams he'd coached to improve and perform above expectations. In Rugby League circles, coaches and players both talk, and all my information said that he could improve players as people and as footballers. His decision to walk away from Brisbane after one season was solely based on not seeing enough of his young family due to the commitment that being at two clubs required.

I understood his reasons.

He continued being successful after several premierships and many representative coaching appointments. Knowing that I'd be coaching Queensland in 2001, I asked him to be involved with the inaugural Emerging State of Origin player concept in 2000. His coaching and rapport with these future

Origin players were exemplified when he included nine players making their State of Origin debuts in the first game of the 2001 series.

Murray was assistant coach at the Cowboys during this time and had to forego his role with me at the end of 2001 when he assumed the head coach role at the club. He didn't believe he could contribute to the Emerging player role as well as coach the Cowboys.

Having his head coaching role at the Cowboys cut short reverberated throughout the country as unfair, and I voiced my opinion of this publicly. Murray agrees now that in this game things do not have to be fair, and decisions are made, some of which defy logic. I wonder if perhaps he was set up to fail. Regardless, I know the events around his demise cut deep with his family.

We've always had a good relationship, even though we don't connect as much as we used to when we first met 30 years ago. Our conversations are hardly ever about Rugby League now, a change I enjoy. Instead, he always speaks of his love for the land. It's almost as though there's something spiritual about these blokes from the bloody big properties in Western Queensland. They can't let it go, and good on them.

I know he grew up quickly with the hardships his family endured: droughts, floods and fluctuating sheep prices. Being lost in the bush as a four-year-old would certainly have affected him, but thankfully, it had a positive effect.

Murray will always have a go at doing something different in his life, and he adapts to roles easily because of his skills with people. That makes him well-suited to his most recent position as Queensland Wellbeing Manager for the National Rugby League (NRL), where his messages and life skills were unmatched. He will always give his best day in, day out. He doesn't need to be the centre of attention – he simply sees himself as an ordinary man who wants to help people. Surprisingly, he had a stint in politics, but he had too much integrity for the level of scrutiny and criticism there.

Murray has dealt with setbacks and – more recently – health issues, but if anyone can come out the other side, it's this bloke.

Wayne Bennett (2021)

Contents

Introduction		1
Chapter 1:	Showdown at the Cowboys	7
Chapter 2:	Floods, Famine and Life on the Land	35
Chapter 3:	Flying High in Business and Politics	61
Chapter 4:	Coaching – Where it Began	75
Chapter 5:	Taking Tonga to the World Cup	91
Chapter 6:	Touring's Memorable Moments	107
Chapter 7:	Coaching, Leadership and Life	125
Chapter 8:	Suicides, Sagas and Social Media	149
Chapter 9:	Parkinson's Disease – the Storm Builds	171
Chapter 10:	What Now?	181
Hear More from Murray		189

Introduction

*"Learn from other people's mistakes.
Life's too short to make them all yourself."*
—adapted from Eleanor Roosevelt

Hello, I'm Murray Hurst. I'm a husband, a father and a former sheep farmer. I've been an airline manager, coached Rugby League in the National Rugby League (NRL) and internationally, and – more recently – held the position of NRL Wellbeing and Education Manager. It's no secret that I was sacked as the coach of the North Queensland Cowboys back in 2002. And I wrote this book to demonstrate how to adjust when your chosen pathways don't materialise and things change when you least expect them to.

That's what happened for me back then.

I grew up on a sheep property in Surat, South West Queensland, then travelled an uncharted (and completely unintended) path through the airline industry, education and construction. Along the way, I fell into professional Rugby League coaching, and the wellbeing and mental health fields.

Through it all, I realised that working in an industry isn't enough. You need to have passion.

I've always believed that when you have a passion for something, you don't need to tell anyone or advertise what that passion is. Instead, passion is something you show through the enthusiasm you display and how you act. My passions, and the directions in which they took me, can easily be seen throughout this memoir.

Growing up on the land as the youngest of five children taught me so many lessons from tough times. I loved the feeling of overcoming the hardships of farming life. Each and every day now, my mind harks back to Wylarah, the property I grew up on. Inevitably, experiences or scenery just come to me.

I never sit down and think, "Oh, I'll give some thought to home." Instead, the memories just come, and there they are.

Funnily, I still call Wylarah 'home' despite not having lived there for 40 years. The place always looked beautiful to me, even during one of the droughts in which we lost nearly 6,000 head of sheep. The constant cycle of transformation from drought to flood seemed to be God-Sent. I know my mother would definitely have believed this.

INTRODUCTION

I couldn't have worked for 18 years in the airline industry either without loving the work, which I did.

Coaching Rugby League is something that I never envisaged for myself, let alone having a defining career in the sport for more than 20 years of coaching against 13 countries. When I rose through the NRL coaching ranks, it just seemed like part of the pathway. I was following my passion. However, the politics of the industry shocked me, and they ultimately led to my sacking.

I also managed wellbeing and education for the NRL in Queensland for more than eight years. I started as the only person doing this in Queensland, then saw my team grow to 17 staff members. This was a clear indication that both the staff and players in Rugby League needed our assistance.

Our team's initial goal was to break down the stigma of talking about wellbeing and mental health in the NRL and Queensland Rugby League. We wanted to address topical issues like drugs, alcohol, gambling, domestic violence and respectful relationships, which are all societal issues as well. And given that players are increasingly becoming role models for younger people, creating a space where they can talk about the issues they face has a wider impact.

Huge expectations have been placed on Rugby League players since the introduction of massive contracts and the transition to suddenly becoming role models. Nothing in their lives growing up prepares the players for how their world will change. No advice their parents gave them covers the situations they'll experience.

On top of this, public perception and the consistent performance levels that large contracts demand contribute to the pressure players experience. To help them cope, the NRL Wellbeing team focuses strongly on growing players' resilience. Passion for the game is essential, but it's no longer enough. Players need a grounding in shared values, openness and respect to maintain both a good game and a good public image.

The most passionate people I've come across while coaching Rugby League are the Tongan Residents. I coached this team for three years and took them to the World Cup. They are also the most respectful people I have met, particularly those who lived in Tonga when I visited. I always wonder why this was the case – no doubt as a result of their upbringing and parenting. Tongan players displayed great resilience too, as you'll see when I talk about them later in this book.

My experiences and the lessons I learnt through all of these roles have proved most beneficial for my work in wellbeing, resilience and mental health. I love people, and it's the people I remember the most when I look back at my career. Passion, resilience and mental toughness stick out in my mind as defining characteristics of those who've both shaped me and been shaped by me over the years.

INTRODUCTION

Now that I've written this memoir, I hope it gives you a different perspective on goals. We tend to think that the value of a goal – short-term, long-term or anything in between – is in achieving it, but sometimes the result is beyond our control. I believe that the value of a goal is in the actions you take to achieve it and the person you become by trying.

I hope that seeing what an ordinary boy from the bush can achieve across various fields without ever setting goals himself will help you to view your own goals differently.

CHAPTER 1

Showdown at the Cowboys

Coaching an NRL side is one of the toughest gigs in sport, and arguably the most cut-throat.

In 2002, what should have been a highlight of my coaching career turned to devastation. I was sacked as head coach of the North Queensland Cowboys in the NRL competition after only three games.

Let me give you some background to set the scene.

Coaching the Cowboys – the early years

The Cowboys were established in Townsville in 1995, and they came under the ownership of News Limited the following year as part of establishing the Super League.

I joined the club in late 1995 to set up and coach the Under-19 team for the 1996 season. I also acted as assistant coach to the highly regarded New Zealander Graham – now Sir

Graham – Lowe, who had a one-year contract as head coach. I even found myself in charge of the first-grade team for several games in 1996 when Graham was absent due to illness.

Then, in 1997, Tim Sheens took over as head coach and I remained as assistant coach. Tim had a fine record as a player and then coach, taking the Canberra Raiders to victory in the 1989, 1990 and 1994 premierships. However, his tenure at the Cowboys was less successful: he quit several games into the 2001 season, claiming he'd been undermined by board members.

Some people claimed that I'd been disloyal to Tim, but I vehemently deny that. I had a great rapport with him and appreciated the trust he showed in me. We had the same thoughts about the game and how it should be played. Tim was a very professional, successful coach who did what he thought was right in all situations. I always spoke highly of him and tried to smooth the way for him with the North Queenslanders, who I felt I understood as a local.

Apart from being Tim's assistant, I also coached the Cowboys' reserve-grade side in 1997–98. We finished second on the competition ladder both years. And despite bowing out in the major semi-finals, we celebrated fine seasons with several players being promoted to first grade.

I finally took over as head coach of the Cowboys in 2001 after Tim quit. The media described the head coach role as the 'toughest job in Rugby League – turning the North Queensland battlers into winners'. However, I was thrilled to have the opportunity to develop a team that I believed could become premiership contenders.

When I took over, the team's results from 1996 to 2000 under Graham and Tim had been mediocre. And, admittedly, they continued to be that way in my first year.

At the time, the directors were well aware of my plans for the team, which I'd outlined in a five-year strategy. I knew that getting the club across the line would take planning, a lot of work and the support of the board. We had to be prepared to sacrifice short-term 'wins' to develop the many talented young players with a view to achieving success down the track.

1997 – the only year of Super League

I was clear from the outset that there would be no quick fix. And at a board meeting in February 2002, board member Paul Travis stood up and stated, "You need to know that all of us are 100% behind you, Murray – no matter what!"

Having always respected people in positions of office, I was elated to hear these words. My belief coming away from that meeting was that at no stage would I need to watch my back.

Things quickly began to change

Just three games (and three losses) into the 2002 season, rumours started floating around that I was to be sacked as head coach.

However, on April 1, an article 'Hurst feels the North Queensland heat as Cowboys' owner lines up Murray' appeared in *The Sydney Morning Herald*, quoting the Cowboys Chief Executive Denis Keeffe. In it, Denis said, "I support Murray Hurst because Murray is coach and I'm chief executive. The coach cops too much blame for things. It's a tough job and I wouldn't do it for a million quid."

But how quickly his views changed.

On April 2, after the Melbourne Storm defeat, I walked from my office to the stadium. I remember the astounded sense of disgust I felt when I was confronted by a new coach – Graham Murray – on the field, talking to the playing group.

I'd never experienced such a sense of disbelief in my life. I know I'd felt disbelief after surviving a head-on collision when

I was 17. And this was the same sort of feeling – except that it would have deep repercussions for my family, not just me.

I was numb. Nobody afforded me the chance to meet with the players to explain what was happening and why. The last time I saw them was when we'd arrived at Townsville Airport from Melbourne the previous day. All this time later, I realise some players probably thought I just walked away and didn't want to confront them.

I found myself back in my office, staring at the ceiling. Nobody at the club had spoken to me regarding what I'd seen, nor what my situation was. Then someone told me to go to the 15th floor of the Casino, Room 1539. There, Frank Stanton – Chief Executive Officer (CEO) of the Cowboys in 2001 and a club executive in 2002 – and Denis Keeffe were waiting.

I don't recall driving there, although I obviously did.

I can't recall everything they said either, but I understood the message that I no longer had a job. Frank was the only one who spoke. God only knows why they couldn't have met me at the club administration building rather than hire out a bloody room at the bloody Ritz.

Hadn't they told me there were budgetary issues?

Then on April 3, again in *The Sydney Morning Herald*, an article headlined 'Hurst Jumps' stated that I'd resigned. Denis said that I'd accepted responsibility for most, if not all, of the team's problems. He claimed, "The board discussed it fully, the arguments were put to Murray today, and he said straight away, 'I resign'."

Rubbish.

It was pure media spin in action. The truth is that Frank had told me that if I didn't resign, I'd be sacked.

A second suggestion – to issue a press release stating that my reason for leaving the club was 'health-related' – was both insulting and a cop-out. I did have health issues – viral meningitis and encephalitis late in 2001, which put me in hospital for a short period. However, I was fit and ready to go for the 2002 season.

I also clearly told Frank that his suggestion that the players had lost faith in me was off the mark. In fact, a lot of players from that team still call me regularly for a chat. It was extremely poor form, but he had to tell me something, I guess…

I later made my feelings known in a letter to him. I'd originally respected him as a successful coach of both Manly and Australia. And when I was first asked to coach the Cowboys, we'd agreed that if he ever had a problem with me, he'd come to me first to discuss things. He certainly wouldn't go to the media about it. We agreed that we'd communicate openly and honestly, as I didn't want my family reading about events in the media without forewarning.

Agreeing to this and then having the reverse happen was a huge disappointment.

The team wasn't doing well that season

A more detailed blow-by-blow analysis of the period shows that cracks had formed, even though I couldn't see them at the time. Hindsight is always 20/20.

For example, the draw for the 2002 season was the toughest the club had encountered, with opening games against the Brisbane Broncos, Newcastle Knights and Melbourne Storm. After leading the Broncos at half-time in Game #1, we were well beaten. The Knights in Game #2 at Newcastle, with the great Andrew Johns as captain, were always going to be tough and they showed why they were the reigning premiers.

And then, the following game in Melbourne against the Storm was fast and furious. So we were beaten again.

On top of all of this, an incident just before the Newcastle game affected our preparation. I'd spent the early part of game day at the hospital, comforting our newly appointed football manager. He'd been assaulted outside a nightclub just after midnight on the day of the game. He and his support staff had asked my permission to go out after dinner. I'd given it, but with the condition that they were home by 11pm.

They weren't.

I arrived back at our accommodation from the hospital just in time to catch the bus to the game. This meant I couldn't run our customary pre-match meeting.

This meeting was essential to ensure that everyone

understood our match plan. It covered where we needed to attack the opposition, plus how we'd deal with their major threats when they have the ball. The meeting was also a time to recognise whether people were focused enough and identify possible red flags. And, of course, it helped to affirm that everyone – the players, coach and group as a whole – was on the same page.

Then, a few hours after our second game of the season against Newcastle, Billy Johnstone – our strength and conditioning coach – told me that I was 'gone'.

Unsurprisingly, this concerned me. Here was someone I'd employed at the start of the season telling me about club decisions and my future that I knew nothing about. It seemed that people were sharing rumblings and rumours about me that I had no way of confirming.

Worse: some of those rumours implied that I'd be sacked.

Even now, I find it hard to believe that I was so naïve that I saw the good in everyone around me. My nature is to trust people. Another lesson learnt: my trust doesn't come cheaply these days.

The days that followed

In the aftermath of my sacking, I had a string of visits – both supportive and less-so. In the days that followed, my visitors told their own story.

I was humbled by both the staff and players who came to

my house to genuinely check on me. People I'd never met came to my home full of anger and disbelief, and I found myself appeasing them. Their appreciation of my endeavours to develop and promote young North Queensland Rugby League players was evident, and my removal angered them. I'd underestimated the support I had in North Queensland and Townsville.

I'll never forget our 16-year-old son Jarrod coming home from school, seeing people everywhere and looking very confused. Meanwhile, our daughter Yana, who was 20 and very mature, was upset and angry.

I also vividly remember front-rower Tim Maddison coming to see me to express his sympathy as I cleaned out my office. "Nice guys run last in this game, Murray," he said. He told Yana, who was helping me, that she should be very proud of me and to look out for me.

She was a great support throughout the whole ordeal.

Meanwhile, board member Laurence Lancini visited me at home the day of my sacking to offer his support. I appreciated this as I have a lot of respect for him. Astonishingly, Laurence knew nothing of my demise until he read it in the newspaper. This probably reflected the governance of the club at the time.

Following the Cowboys debacle, the support I received from other NRL clubs, Cowboys supporters and the media around the country and overseas was overwhelming.

Wayne Bennett, the most successful coach in Rugby League

history, threw his support behind me. After having endorsed me to become the Cowboys' long-term coach in 2001, he spoke out after my sacking. In one newspaper interview, he said, "If Murray Hurst was incompetent in some way, then by God, the administrators have been as well."

Catching up with Wayne Bennett in Townsville in 2010

Looking at coaches who influenced my career, Wayne is the obvious No #1 – he had fantastic people skills and could always get the best from players he coached. Although, granted, I also recognise Tim Sheens as a Rugby League innovator and a teacher for budding coaches. He was forever devising new methods and techniques for players to improve their game and their teamwork in general.

Wayne and I have kept in touch through everything. I often say about friends, "You don't have to see them every day, every week or even every year. But when you do catch up, nothing changes – you just pick up where you left off."

Wayne is a perfect example of this. He cares about people.

The visits weren't just to me, either. They say there is often a loving bond between father and daughter, and this is still the case with Yana and me.

So, the following day, Yana drove to the Cowboys office and demanded a meeting with Frank Stanton. To his credit, he met with her – and when she left, he commented, "That is a very strong young lady there."

But nothing she said changed anything, of course. I was the 'fall guy': the one they blamed and got rid of as a publicity stunt to cover whatever dealings were happening behind the scenes.

And as if the anguish of the situation wasn't enough, on the afternoon of my sacking, a board member who was a solicitor approached me. He warned me not to sue for unfair dismissal because the owner of the club, News Ltd, had deep pockets. He assured me it would be a David versus Goliath contest if I tried.

He didn't realise that morally, I'd never have taken that path anyway.

The reality was that if the Cowboys hadn't gone on to develop the way I expected them to, I truly *would* have put my hand up and walked. However, I was confident that, with my philosophies and previous coaching success, the club would develop into a major force.

> "Failure is not the worst thing in the world. The very worst is not to try.
>
> Failure is the opportunity to start again, more intelligently."
>
> —adapted from Henry Ford

Every club has a different dynamic

Sometimes, I look back, amazed at the state of the coaching team in the lead-up to my departure.

Support staff are often the make-or-break members for a team's chances in a league. Broadcaster, administrator, former player and coach Phil Gould has said that the St George Dragons burnt talented young coaches Nathan Brown and Paul McGregor. He claimed they'd both been set up for failure by their support staff's lack of experience.

Thinking back, I realise I'd had no support staff at all when I took over as the Cowboys' head coach. Tim Sheens' staff had all departed the club with him, so I was a one-man band. I just accepted that at the time, but I can see now that it was a ridiculous situation to be in at the NRL level.

For my entire first year, I didn't have a football manager, an assistant coach, a strength and conditioning coach, a trainer or even an administration person. The board told me that the club couldn't afford any support staff, even though Tim had had a full (presumably paid) support team.

My only help to train, coach and turn the team around from years of losses was from John Alloway, a PE teacher at St Ignatius Park College. John wrote and supervised our strength and conditioning, but could only work before and after school hours.

Regardless, he was still a great help to me. He'd assisted with several clubs and representative teams I'd previously coached, including Tonga in the World Cup and the Australia Under-17, and was very trustworthy and knowledgeable.

Then, during my second year, I had a full-time strength and conditioning coach (Billy Johnstone), an assistant coach (Happy Thomson) and a football manager (Peter Parr). But all the other positions remained unfilled. And it's probably telling that Graham Murray, who replaced me, brought in five support staff – which is the norm in the NRL.

I also realised over time that I should have negotiated a stronger, more rewarding contract with the Cowboys. I later learnt that my replacement coach was paid seven times my salary.

Ironically, back when I was appointed, I would have done the job for nothing – more fool me.

I received a lot of support from the players

Only days before I departed the Cowboys, a player who asked to remain anonymous was quoted in the media as saying that I trained the team, "… like a kindergarten side… We're like little kids running around." He claimed that I didn't have confidence in myself and that I had a few players offside.

After finding out who it was, I wasn't surprised, but I will say I was disappointed. I think it's gutless to criticise someone in the media without putting your name to the comments.

Criticism – especially in the media – can often create self-doubt about your methods.

Despite this, however, I was confident that I was on the right track with the Cowboys.

Meanwhile, Paul Bowman – the Cowboys centre at the time – said in the same article, "If anyone is accountable, it's the players. The things that are getting us into trouble are one-on-one tackles. There's nothing wrong with what Murray's doing."

I felt that Paul's comments reflected his maturity, and I wasn't surprised that he went on to play 203 games for the Cowboys, as well as captaining the side. He also played 12 State of Origin games for Queensland and achieved a sports science degree while playing at the top level. As I write this, he's still with the Cowboys as head of sports science.

I've kept in touch with Paul since those days. And recently, I asked him to share his thoughts on his early years at the Cowboys – the only club he's ever played for during his distinguished professional career.

Paul Bowman's early years at the Cowboys

"It's probably an understatement to say my career as a professional Rugby League player was at a crossroads when I first met Murray Hurst. In November 1995, the Cowboys had assembled a new coaching team – Graham Lowe as head coach for the 1996 season before Tim Sheens

arrived in 1997. The assistant coaches were former New Zealand captain Mark Graham and Murray Hurst.

"I played most of my career at around 98 kg. When I arrived at the Cowboys in March 1995, I think I weighed 88 kg. I'd never done any strength training through school, so I focused on this during the 1995 season. It definitely helped me increase my weight – as did overindulgence in the wrong foods – and I turned up to pre-season training in November weighing 106 kg!

"Being overweight led to groin and back issues during the pre-season, and inevitably led to my non-selection in the first-grade side for the start of the 1996 season. I also missed selection in the reserve-grade team, so my 1996 season started in the Under-19 side, coached by Murray Hurst.

"At the time, I took no responsibility for my actions. I was the incumbent first-grade centre from the season before and felt I deserved selection. I believed that what had happened was more about personality issues and the new staff not rating me as a player. Of course, experience now tells me that the fault lay clearly at my feet. I regret speaking negatively about any coach or staff at the time because if I'd been in their shoes, I would've done exactly the same thing.

"So that gives some context to where I found myself in 1996 and my first recollection of Murray. My career was at

a crossroads: I'd gone from being the Cowboys incumbent first-grade centre to not being able to make reserve grade. I had to play in the Under-19 side when I wasn't even under 19 – I turned 20 in 1996! The Under-19 side was made up of the Cowboys' best junior players. So, after playing first grade the year before, playing in that team really felt like a slap in the face.

"That year was also a tumultuous period at the Cowboys because we were having little success. As a player, I found it a constant struggle. Yet I never saw Murray show anything but integrity, honesty and loyalty to the club. The coaching staff and I all had a great relationship with him during the tough times on the field.

"The thing I remember most was that he was honest with me when I found myself in the Under-19 team. He was honest about how I'd let myself down with my pre-season training condition, but also honest about being happy to have me in the side. He believed in my ability at a time when I was probably starting to doubt it. He told me I had to work hard, play to my potential and be an example to the younger players in the team.

"I now look back on the days in that team as some of the most enjoyable times I've had in football. The team had a close bond, which reflected on the coach and the culture he instilled. Murray helped to put me back on the right path. His guidance led me back to reserve grade and then into first grade for the last part of the 1996 season. I'm thankful for his honesty and loyalty.

"He also showed plenty of loyalty to other players from North Queensland, nurturing the likes of Matty Bowen, John Doyle, Nathan Fien, John Buttigieg, Scott Donald and Scott Prince – North Queensland juniors and future State of Origin representatives. Murray laid the foundations of future success for them by developing them through the early 2000s.

"To Murray, Thanks for making me a better footballer and better person."
–Paul Bowman

"Finally, during his time coaching the Cowboys from 1995 to early 2002, Murray showed a great work ethic. In fact, everyone who knew him worried that his desire for workplace perfection sometimes affected his health. I remember some training sessions of three-plus hours in the Under-19 side. At the time I didn't enjoy them, but I could see they came from his drive for perfection."

Objectives for the team

I was totally confident that my knowledge, methods and personality would succeed at top-level coaching. For example, I knew that Rugby League demands that players get off the ground time and time again after either being hit hard in tackles or making tackles themselves. This doesn't happen just once or twice in any given set, but three or even four times.

Quickly getting back up off the ground and into a defensive position again is paramount for all players. So if the Cowboys could improve this aspect, our players could take advantage in attack and win games. This meant that having the fastest 'off-the-ground' speed rapidly became the goal.

As is always the case, a new coach works with several players that the outgoing coach brought to the club. I believe I got on well with all the Cowboys players since I'd already worked with them as assistant coach. Even so, some players probably still had a strong allegiance to Tim Sheens as he'd valued them enough to employ them.

Meanwhile, several players were off-contract at the end of the 2001 season, so recruiting new blood was critical. And it was up to me to identify replacements. I thought this would be quite easy as there were plenty of players willing to follow me to the Cowboys.

However, my joy was short-lived when Frank Stanton told me that the club had no money for new players. I wanted to sign a couple of players of note as prospective first graders, but I was told that it just wasn't possible.

The 2002 season really was akin to starting with a new, completely inexperienced group of players. Many of the previous members had departed the club for reasons that included contracts running out, lack of funds to re-sign, poaching from other clubs, long-term injuries and retirements.

I accepted this: as I've always said, it's no good worrying about who you haven't got. Additionally, I believed I had the backing of the board.

Eventually, however, I did get enough money for two major signings. One was Matt Sing, an established try-scoring first grader that I'd known since his childhood days. He'd represented Queensland in State of Origin and Australia. The other person of note wasn't a current player. Rather, it was strength and conditioning coach Billy Johnstone, whom I mentioned earlier in the chapter. He'd also played top-grade Rugby League and had been a professional boxer.

When I took over, I thought the Cowboys players lacked mental toughness. For example, in previous seasons, they'd shown that they could be competitive for 50 to 60 minutes, but then they'd collapse in the final quarter. I could see that it was due to a lack of fitness and concentration, which equated to a lack of mental toughness. This had become well known to opposition teams, who capitalised on the weakness.

I also believed that breeding toughness and resilience into

the team would take two to three years. So our goal became to lessen or even eliminate the 1:1 missed tackles. To do this, the players needed strength, very good technique and awareness. And I believed that Billy would be the ideal person to help them with this.

Meanwhile, I desperately wanted to introduce young North Queensland players such as Sam Thaiday to the Cowboys to develop them. I was devastated to hear that we didn't have the money to sign Sam – it would have cost only $500 per year to keep him on a scholarship. As it was, he went on to forge an outstanding career with the Broncos, Queensland in State of Origin, and Australia.

We'd also previously lost Scott Prince, Scott Donald, Mark Shipway and Nathan Fien in similar circumstances. Scott Prince had played over 300 NRL games, won a premiership and represented Queensland and Australia. Nathan had played over 270 NRL games, won a premiership and represented Queensland and New Zealand. Scott Donald played nearly 250 NRL and Super League games and broke try-scoring records in England and Australia. Mark played 170 NRL and Super League games.

Additionally, both Scotts and Nathan were North Queenslanders, and I know that they'd rather have played in their own backyard. The four of them could have given the Cowboys such an advantage to achieve success.

At least they're now all successful people in their chosen fields.

Rapport with players is key to successful coaching

The support I received from senior players from the day I took over as head coach was heartening. The support from younger and new players to the club was even more so. And 20 years later, I still have a strong relationship with many of the players and their families.

I attribute this to being very honest with them from the beginning and right throughout our relationship, including both the downtimes and the commendation times. Put simply, if people understood my values and my rigidity around those values, they learnt that abiding by your beliefs in all situations is good for your soul.

Over the years, I've noticed that many players exhibit actions to prove this theory.

As an example of the support I received, our club's most experienced player, Tim Brasher, came to my office quite often to build my confidence. He knew that I'd been a successful coach at various levels and assumed that my confidence was suffering from how the media portrayed me. By the end of his career, Tim had played 16 tests for Australia, 21 State of Origin games and 244 first-grade matches. He'd been around a long time and had seen many predicaments with clubs, so he noticed a lot.

Even though he was at the end of his career, he helped greatly by affirming my methods. He always came to my office before training sessions to check what we were doing in the session. This way, he could support everything I said and all that I wanted the players to do.

I also had a lot of respect for Julian O'Neill, who gave me the impression he'd do whatever was needed for the team to improve and work toward success. Julian's career included 361 first-grade games and 10 State of Origins. He also played for Australia.

Then there was our captain, Paul Bowman, whom I already mentioned above. Paul respected me and my achievements, and desperately wanted the Cowboys to succeed. After the last game against the Melbourne Storm, Paul had given so much that he couldn't get off the dressing room floor to accompany me to the press conference.

It was this kind of resilience that I wanted to cultivate in all my players.

But cultivating resilience and toughness in players is a two-way street. While I asked a lot of them both in training and on the field, I also supported them in all their endeavours. And they truly repaid my efforts later on.

For example, I mentioned signing Matt Sing earlier. Matt was a man of very few words, preferring to lead with action.

But if he had something to say during training or at half-time in games, everyone gave him their total attention. We had a short history of coaching, but he still surprised me with his empathy and support when I was shown the door.

Just as important to me was the overwhelming support I received from younger players who I had brought to the club and spent many hours developing.

To have men like John Doyle, John Buttigieg, John Manning, Matty Bowen, Paul Dezolt and Paul Pensini show empathy and have my back meant a lot to me. These players had all come through to first grade from North Queensland junior Rugby League with Doyley, Butts and Matty going on to play State of Origin.

Micheal Luck was another player we brought through the development pathway and he finished with over 200 first-grade games with the Cowboys and Warriors. He was identified from a state Under-15 carnival, along with Chris Muckert, who also went on to play frequent first grade. Micheal is now Chief Operating Officer of the Cowboys.

Yet another player who really stood out for me was John Doyle: one of the toughest, most skilful players I've coached. I brought him to the Cowboys from Rockhampton as a skinny 69 kg five-eighth. His natural strength was something I hadn't seen up until then, and haven't seen since.

John just loved to take on the biggest opponent, but his sheer physicality in tackles was sometimes detrimental to both himself and the team. I used to joke that he looked in the mirror and saw a 2 m, 110 kg MMA fighter – much like a chihuahua might look in a mirror and see a Great Dane! I encouraged him to put on more muscle without losing his agility, something he needed to direct play from the hooking position.

John then went on to play NRL and State of Origin at 95 kg due to his commitment to gym work. One of my strengths was building rapport with players to bring them through to play at a higher level, no matter where I coached. I could somehow build their confidence, improve their skills and make them better people.

Overall impressions of my time with the Cowboys

Looking back over what I've learnt, I believe that whenever someone departs an organisation of their own accord and without burning bridges, there's no animosity. When the organisation makes the decision unilaterally, though, there's always an element of disbelief.

While the seven years I spent at the Cowboys was much shorter than I'd hoped for, I have fond memories of the people there and the fun we had. I was mostly happy with what we did in that time, and pleased with the number of young players who made careers out of the sport. I'd always aspired to be a head coach, but had never expected it to come the way it did.

Throughout my time there, Tim Sheens was very good to me, and I learnt so much from him. We got on very well and I miss our chats.

The sacking was a definite kick in the guts, as I was still in the early stages of my five-year plan to win a premiership at that point. And the Cowboys *did* win one in four years, so good on them.

Regardless, the numbness set in immediately. And really, I don't think it subsided for a couple of years. I had no plans for moving forward beyond it: a good reminder NOT to put all your eggs in one basket, I guess.

But over the years, as dark thoughts have come along, simply thinking of my family has usually been enough to buck me out of them.

Since this career-defining moment, I've been able to look back at the gifts coaching has given me. I made good friends and gained lifelong supporters. It's heartening that people have since told me they remembered me saying this or that to them.

Moving forward after events such as this isn't easy, but I know that being strong, unselfish and resilient is a good recipe. Sometimes I think I'd never have bounced back and tried different things if I hadn't had the resilience I'd inherited from life on the land.

Never forget where you came from.

On Shaky Ground

Calm hands take control of turbulent Cowboys

HE'S THE MAN!

Bennett backs Cowboys' new coach

SUPERCOACH Wayne Bennett (inset) says new Cowboys coach Murray Hurst is the right man for the toughest job in rugby league — turning the North Queensland battlers into winners.

Bennett said chasing a high-profile coach might not be the Cowboys' best move and Hurst (pictured at training) — the man he will face in today's NRL clash — was up to the challenge.

• Full report, Page 124

Hurst right for the job: Benny

SHOWDOWN AT THE COWBOYS

CHAPTER 2

Floods, Famine and Life on the Land

There are precious few things you can trust on the land.

When I look back on my childhood in the 1960s, I realise what an incredible upbringing I had. Our family sheep station – 'Wylarah' – was near Surat in outback Queensland. I was the youngest of the five Hurst children, with three sisters – Donella, Peta and Terry – and one brother, Hilton. And all of us thought we were the only people in the world due to the remoteness as we helped our parents tend to our flock of over 12,000 sheep.

Family was the cornerstone of our existence.

I suppose when you're diagnosed with a life-impacting disease like Parkinson's, your emotional ties to childhood take on greater clarity. Not that I've ever forgotten the wonderful times, nor the hardship during droughts and floods, that I experienced while growing up with my family. Even now, 44 years after leaving the property, I still refer to Wylarah as 'home'. I can never overestimate the ways in which growing up there prepared me, both physically and mentally, for the challenges I've faced in my life.

I want to tell you some tales of growing up on the land out there in outback Queensland. They'll give you an idea of the kind of experiences that bred me into the man I am today. Life on the property was harsh and not always fair. I certainly had to toughen up fast, but it was also beautiful and that's much the way I see life now.

The homestead at Wylarah Station where we all grew up

The Hurst siblings: Donella, Peta, Terry, Hilton and Murray

My family history

My great-great-grandfather was a self-redeeming convict who was sent over from England in the 1800s for highway robbery. As his descendent, I was destined to inherit an element of resilience and a very strong work ethic. After arriving at Botany Bay, he was sent west to Penrith at the base of the Blue Mountains to become a policeman.

Dad's father served in both the First and Second World Wars, and was shot three times. He died, aged 49, of tuberculosis. My father was one of seven children – each child born in between the wars.

On my mother's side, I am the grandson of a man whose family settled the land around the Surat and Maranoa district in the early 1900s. Most of the land was sold to people who wanted to grind out a living producing cattle, wheat and sheep. Our family were sheep farmers, with cattle as a backup.

Lawrence Simpson, my grandfather, owned the business L.A. Simpson & Co. which incorporated three properties – Rewfarm, Wylarah and Yanco. When my grandfather died, he left Wylarah to my parents and his other two properties to his son Barry. My great-grandfather's name – Alex Simpson – still serves as the numbers on the Shire Hall clock.

Mum had her five children in just over four years, none of them twins. How would mothers of today manage this without electricity? I was the baby of the brood, and Dad said that at the time she was feeding me, she was also feeding 18 lambs and two poddy calves. Of course, I was the only one on the breast though.

We often had to raise orphaned lambs or poddy calves whose mothers had died while giving birth or been killed by foxes. Joey kangaroos were also part of the family: we always seemed to adopt them after shooting their mothers or after they'd been hit by cars on the main road.

There was often a snake problem or infestation around the homestead too. Mum killed 11 browns one day at the bottom of our back stairs. Two of them would have been at least 6 feet long, while the others – just babies – were about 2 feet.

The beginnings of resilience

I developed a passion for work through spending time with Dad. You don't quit as a kid on a farming property. When things fall apart, you pick yourself up and start again.

So I credit this as being where I learnt my first lessons in resilience.

I remember having a traumatic experience as a four-year-old when I got lost in the seemingly endless expanse of the property. Even at that young age, I was expected to do my bit whenever I accompanied Dad to wherever work needed to be done.

My sister Terry was also with us that day. We were mustering a few hundred head of sheep and herding them into the sheepyards for drenching. We'd divided them into a couple of separate groups. Once they began to follow a fence or sensed that other sheep were going in the same direction as them, they'd all stay together and walk in the same direction.

I was supposed to follow a herd of sheep back to the yards for drenching, but I somehow lost contact with them. I was terrified of being alone, worried that I might be attacked by a wild pig. I wandered for hours in the great emptiness before eventually being found many miles from where I should have been.

I recall suddenly seeing Dad running toward me and Terry standing behind him in tears. The sheep had done the right thing, but I'd let Dad down. Who knows what would have happened had I not been found.

In a strange way, I think this may have hardened me up somewhat. Later, at age eight, I'd camp out on my own overnight with my dog and a rifle. I would shoot roos at night, having become quite good after going shooting with Dad and my siblings.

We treated those shooting expeditions like a family outing. Mum would have warm toast in the oven for when we returned home. We loved it.

From around that age to when I left the property, I used to help Dad skin the roos we'd shot. We'd stretch the skins out and peg them onto the ground in the chook-yard. Then, when they dried, we'd take them into town and get paid for them – either by weight or size of the skin.

If we presented a pig's snout and tail to the council, they would pay us two shillings. Meanwhile, a fox scalp brought five shillings. The council offered this bounty because these animals were pests,

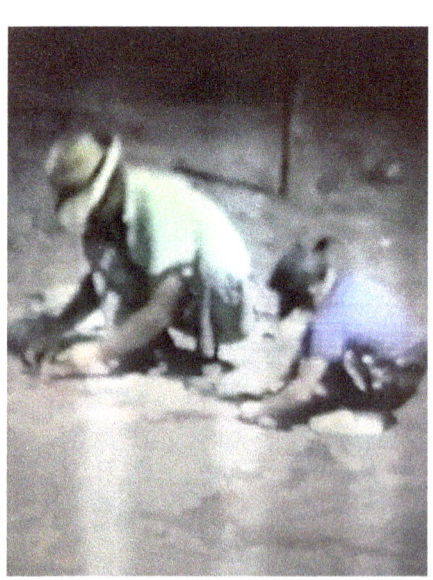

Dad and I pegging kangaroo skins in 1964

as were rabbits. Interestingly, my grandfather had actually made a living from these tasks in between fighting in the First and Second World Wars. At that time, we could also sell rabbits for their meat.

As an eight-year-old in 1965, I also helped Dad to skin hundreds of dead sheep during a severe drought. That was a life experience that truly built my resilience. Dad obviously skinned many more than I did, but at that stage in life, my effort was pretty good.

I'd drive the ute and pull up beside the dead ones, skin them and throw the skins in the back. I spent many a night in tears but it was a gruesome job that had to be done. We only got a few pence for each skin but it helped us survive. We lost over 6,000 head of sheep during that drought – a depressing time.

I remember on one occasion, Dad sold around 600 head of sheep for 40 pence (40 cents) each. These days a single leg of lamb is over $30.00, which would have been an unimaginable sum in those times.

The harsh realities of life on the land were evident in other areas. During wet weather, parasitic flies would lay eggs on the soggy wool of the sheep. After hatching, the maggots would bury themselves in the fleece and eventually under the sheep's skin, feeding off the flesh. We had to treat affected sheep quickly or they'd end up with exposed patches of red raw flesh.

The good news is that the treatment really worked. I saw sheep that had had their entire back infested with hundreds of maggots. After being dipped to kill the maggots, the sheep would arrive at the shearing shed a couple of months later with no scars or evidence that they'd ever been fly-blown.

I recall once finding a ram that had a cracked skull from butting heads with another ram and maggots coming out of his ears and eyes. We treated him with dip, and after wiring up his horns to keep his skull together, he was as good as gold.

Sheep are incredibly resilient: they can survive on virtually nothing. When food was scarce on our property, they'd eat cactus and prickly pear, leaving them with spines in their mouth and skin. We often cut down Bauhinia trees for additional food for sheep too. They'd hear the chainsaw start up and come from miles around, knowing they'd find something to eat. Amazingly, some sheep would start moving toward the noise of the chainsaw but be too weak to reach us and would drop dead on the way.

And now, when I think of that time, I can see how the patience of waiting for the dip to work has led me to patience for the long game in other areas of life. It's a patience that you can't pretend to have, and one that I only see in people who've been on the land.

Crutching was our preferred method of preventing the sheep from becoming fly-blown. It was necessary because their urine would wet the wool, allowing flies to lay eggs that would hatch as maggots. This work was carried out by shearers.

We'd muster our sheep around six months after they had

been shorn, which was also six months before their next shear. Crutching the ewes involved shearing their rear-ends and down their back legs. Crutching the wethers (which are really castrated rams) involved shearing the wool around their bellies, which became wet when they urinated.

Shearers would also treat any fly-blown sheep as they crutched them. We preferred crutching to the far less humane mulesing, which involved actually removing skin from the sheep's rear-end, and which I believe is now outlawed.

We ate what we farmed or caught

Speaking of flies, roast lamb was a favourite meal for all of us and one that we never became 'fed up with', so to speak. Regardless of whether the meal was lunch or dinner, there would always be flies hovering in the kitchen as we didn't have screens. After we'd enjoyed our meals – eating everything on the plate as we'd been taught – we'd invariably see each plate ringed with dead flies that had landed in the gravy. We simply pushed them to the rim of the plate and carried on eating. These days most families panic if they discover an insect of some sort in their house.

I was never shielded from anything by my parents and, as a result, I grew up very quickly. When we had visitors to the property, Dad would often tell me to slip down to the paddock and get a wether. I'd bring it back, slit its throat, help Dad 'dress' it, and give it to our visitor. I also learnt to use Dad's guns from an early age and I'd shoot rabbits, skin them, cook them and take them to school for lunch.

We used to catch wild pigs and fatten them as a variation in our diet from mutton. I loved eating the pig's eyes. We'd also kill a couple of sheep a week for family consumption. My favourite portion was the brains, which I'd scoop out of the head and boil along with the tongue. We were always told to eat everything on our plate at every meal and even ask for more if we weren't full. This became a habit that I found hard to get out of as I grew older!

An annual event I remember vividly was the lambing season in which all lambs needed to be 'marked'. Their tails were

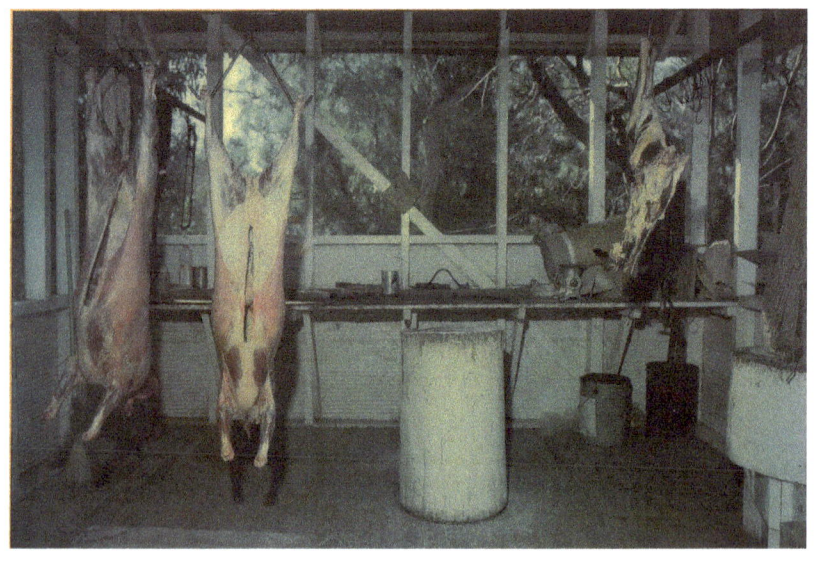

We would cool the sheep overnight in the Meat House in readiness for processing

lopped, ears punched with our brand, and if they were male they were castrated.

Once, when Dad was carrying out a castration, he dropped the instrument he was using to pull out the testicles. Rather than pick up the instrument, he pulled out the testicles with his teeth and spat them out. That was all good except when he spat them out his false teeth went with the testicles. He picked up his teeth, put them on a rail and carried on!

Normality growing up

I recall two milestones while I was at Surat State School. One was the advent of decimal currency replacing pounds, shillings and pence on February 14, 1966. The other was when humans first walked on the moon on July 20, 1969. My class gathered at the bank manager's residence to watch the moon landing because he had one of the few television sets in town.

If we weren't driven to school, we'd catch the bus from our mailbox on the Surat–St George road, two miles from the homestead. Well, it wasn't technically a bus – it was a Kombi van. The driver, Claude Crane, was fairly ordinary (by which I mean 'bloody terrible'). He once rolled the van with us in it because he didn't see the piles of gravel that the council had put on the road to spread out for repair. There were also times in the wet season when our property was flooded. During those days, we had to walk from the homestead to the main road to catch the bus to school as the black soil made roads impassable.

As a child, I loved driving our ute around the property, and by the age of 12, I had ventured out onto the open road. At this young age, I was also playing A-grade cricket for Surat and often travelled hundreds of kilometres to play a game. In fact, my cricketing love started when I was ten.

A bloke called Venn Minnage, who was captain of the A grade, used to come to the school to show us the fundamentals. I used to drive 16 miles twice a week to train. My preference was batting in those days, but I became more of a bowler as I matured. Some days, my mate Sid would bowl to me out on the property for almost the whole day. I was forever listening to Alan McGilvray calling test matches in Australia or England through the night, and I bought cricket magazines whenever they were released.

Some of the seasoned guys in our cricket team would go to the pub after the game while I'd wait in one of their cars, often for several hours. When they were ready to leave, they'd toss me the keys and tell me I was driving. I finished grade 10 at Surat by driving myself to school in the family ute. I was 14.

Three years later, when I was 17 and eligible to get a driver's licence, the police in Surat simply wrote out a licence for me, saying they'd seen me driving around for several years.

I also remember the Balonne River flowing through the back of our property. In flood, it would join with the lagoon near our homestead. To rescue sheep during floods, we'd put five or six

The mailbox at Wylarah at the turn-off to the property from the main road joining Surat and St George

in our rowboat and then drop them to dry land. Sometimes, this would be a daylight-to-dark exercise.

Once when I was 12, though, I had to swim through the torrent to where some sheep were stranded. I was exhausted because I was wearing heavy, army-type boots that strapped halfway up my shins. Seeing a log floating toward me in the current, I heaved myself onto it, only to discover a death adder glaring at me. He was taking a free ride and a rest as well.

Needless to say, I let him have the log.

Another job I took on was working as a roustabout in the shearing shed. This involved eight-hour days spent picking up fleeces off the floor. We'd throw them onto a large 'wool-classers' table for the piece-pickers to pull apart and toss the standards into different bins for pressing. These were big days when you had six shearers to pick up for.

Most shearing sheds were six-stand sheds. This meant that there was room for six shearers operating together. A good shearer would reach 200 sheep in a day, so you can imagine how busy that would keep the roustabout. But being paid $10 a day made it all worthwhile.

I was 16 when we eventually had electricity connected. Before then, I'd felt so sorry for Mum having to do the washing in a copper pot in the backyard. Ironing required heating up two or three irons at one time on the stove to keep them hot. She'd also spend hours making a cake or biscuits and baking them in our wood-fired oven, only to see them devoured in two minutes by five hungry children after they arrived home from school.

Religious faith was instilled in the Hurst children from an early age. Mum was a staunch Catholic who would take us to Mass each Sunday. Dad wasn't as serious about religion as Mum, though. He once told me that if you could live with your conscience, that was Christian enough. When I finished my primary schooling in Surat, I went to Marist College Ashgrove in Brisbane as a boarder. During grade 12, I was actually serious about becoming a priest. But, in the end, the lure of the land was too great. I wanted to get back out to the property to help Dad.

I'm still serious about religion although I'd never force it on anyone. But I believe my faith has carried me through the tough times in my life.

Life, death and adventure in between

When I think about growing up in Surat, it seems that I did a lot of shooting, fishing and other adventuresome activities – and I guess I did. Some of it may seem hard – even callous – by today's standards, but back then it was just what you did. I learnt it from my dad, and that's what it took to make a living and survive on the land. Nowadays, my wife Pam says I'm an absolute softy. And it's true: I couldn't even hit a dog these days; I'm so sooky with them.

It's amazing how things change.

My best mate growing up at Surat was Russell (Sid) Mundy – the boy who'd come over to the property to bowl for me. He belonged to a large Aboriginal family from the Mandandanji people, whom everyone in town treated respectfully. Every weekend, Sid and I would spend whole days shooting, fishing, camping out or playing sport of some kind. Occasionally, we'd have to help Dad mustering sheep or fixing fences.

Surprisingly, Sid was afraid of two things: the dark and snakes. I recall once we were fishing and camping on the riverbank and had several lines set to catch cod and yellowbelly. Checking the lines several times during the night, and with only a carbide lamp light to see with, Sid would walk so close behind me that he'd stand on my heels in fear of being bitten by a snake.

When the Balonne River was in flood the year I was 13, Hilton, Sid and I were swimming above the weir at Surat. The water was flowing about nine inches deep over the weir and we noticed that fish were being washed over, so we decided to try to catch some by hand. We boxed in the area on the concrete levee slab where the water met the bank with logs so that if fish crossed here, they couldn't escape. We'd caught several yellowbelly when, suddenly, this big cod emerged from the flood water and flopped at my feet.

People may not know how big the Murray cod can grow, but the biggest Dad ever brought home was 88lbs. We caught a 62lb cod in the Balonne River once too. On the day I was with Hilton and Sid, I picked up the cod at my feet by forcing a hand in each of its gills, then ran up the bank. Dad was at the pub at the time, so we took it in to show him. It weighed 45lbs and remained in the pub's cold room for a week so that locals could have a look after hearing the story.

The 45lb Murray cod I caught with my hands in 1971

In those days I shot many rabbits, pigs and kangaroos. At one time, we introduced myxomatosis to our properties to eradicate the fast-breeding rabbits. We administered it by catching rabbits, injecting them with the virus and then releasing them. They'd go blind and die because they couldn't source food, which was very cruel. After this, we introduced liquid 1080 poison, which we poured down rabbit burrows. When the rabbits entered, they'd get the poison on their paws and later clean them by licking the poison off, thus killing them. We lost a couple of dogs through this: they'd often chase rabbits into the burrows and therefore get the poison on their own paws.

Sid and I would often shoot at night with a spotlight attached to the battery of the ute. Sid was a poor shot, so I did most of the shooting. One Saturday on Wylarah, we were shooting pigs: me with a .303 rifle and Sid with a .22. I accidentally shot one of our dogs, Lassie (a kelpie), through the neck.

The bullet had ricocheted off a branch in front of the pig, entered Lassie's neck and passed through. She was losing a lot of blood as I carried her a couple of miles back to the ute. When I arrived home, I injected her with penicillin and stitched her up with fishing line. I knew I'd be in strife with Dad, as he needed her on Sunday to muster sheep for shearing on Monday.

The next morning, I was amazed to see Lassie following Dad on his horse to go mustering with the other dogs. Kelpies are tough dogs. And yes, I did tell Dad what had happened. He just told me to learn from it.

I really can't remember how many dogs we had over time on the property. The hardest thing was having to put down a dog that had been such a great worker in both the paddock and the shearing shed. Dad mostly did this, but as I got older, it seemed to be my responsibility. We put them down for reasons of injury or age, or even not being able to grasp the working-dog ethic.

The only dog that Dad couldn't shoot was his best dog over 10–12 years – old Dixie. He was so upset at her deterioration that he asked me to do it for him. She'd produced nine litters of pups by that point, and I guess she meant more to him than to me at the time.

The toughest and most emotional time I had putting down an animal was with my horse. She was a young filly who'd been running with a racehorse stallion we had. Unfortunately, she'd been ruptured by the stallion and, by the time we found her, her back end was infested with maggots. Putting the rifle to her forehead and putting her out of her misery was devastating.

As I've said, it is tough on the land.

Sid and I grew apart for a while after I left to board at Marist College Ashgrove. The year I finished school, I came back to the property to help Dad. I played A grade for Surat in the Western Downs Rugby League team, which included the four Mundy brothers – Sid, Ross, Jock and Bobby. They were all very good players.

We won the premiership that year against St George. The competition included Surat, St George, Dirranbandi and Mungindi. I recall travelling from Surat to Mungindi in the back of a ute, then playing two games against Mungindi after the five-hour trip.

The return journey was long, and after being dropped off at the turn-off to Wylarah at 2am then walking two miles home, I had to help Dad muster sheep at 6am. It's just what you had to do. That was a tough competition with most players being shearers, ringers or from properties.

We had a representative team that year that beat Toowoomba, who had beaten Cronulla in the Amco Cup. That was a mid-week competition that included ARL (Australian Rugby League) and divisional teams.

Setbacks

In 1974, at the age of 17, I decided to leave the property for a couple of years and go to Rockhampton, where my brother and two of my sisters were then living. I wanted to play A-grade cricket in Rockhampton, and in 1975, I was selected to play for Queensland Country against Pakistan. There were some great names in that Pakistan side – Zaheer Abbas, Intikhab Alam and Majid Khan to name just a few. I managed to pick up a couple of wickets with my right-arm off-breaks.

The following year, I got to bowl against legendary English cricketer Geoff Boycott, who was holding batting clinics in Queensland. He was apparently impressed with my bowling because I dismissed him three times during an exhibition batting display on a turf wicket.

Afterwards, at a function where he was guest speaker, he sounded me out about a contract with his county cricket club Yorkshire in England. We actually chatted for a couple of hours. While this was exciting, I thought it was merely Boycott giving a young fellow some encouragement.

Surprisingly, a few weeks later, a letter arrived from Boycott confirming the invitation for me to play for Yorkshire. A bank job and accommodation were included. I was devastated when I severely injured my knee in a Rugby League game and couldn't make the commitment. This resulted in my first knee reconstruction, which put me in rehabilitation for eight months.

I think my parents were secretly pleased I couldn't go, and my siblings were generally in the 'oh well' mode. Little did I know that it would be the first of several operations from Rugby League I'd have. Being young, I was quite devastated – both with not going overseas and not being able to play Rugby League for some time.

My way of managing was to put everything into my work and focus on the good things in my life. Looking back, I'd been very chuffed at the prestige associated with being basically plucked from oblivion and given an opportunity like that.

I'd always intended to return to Wylarah to work and live the rest of my life. However, my dream was shattered in 1976 when my parents had to sell due to drought. Well, it wasn't only due to drought. There were three neighbouring properties involved with the smallest being Wylarah, which didn't even have its own shearing shed. It did have the best water supply, but Dad was still disappointed that the others had been left to my uncle.

For the previous 15 years, Dad had worked and managed the three properties and everything to do with the company. So to only be left the one was devastating. Then the drought forced the decision of moving to Rockhampton, which was an enormous step as it is for country people.

My sister Terry, Hilton and I had been living in Rockhampton for a while at that point, so Mum and Dad moved and bought a house there. Being in suburbia, Mum felt like everyone was watching her and wouldn't go outside for quite a while. Dad worked at Hastings Deering. I felt sorry for them having to experience the unintended lifestyle change, and I don't think they ever really got over it.

Personally, Wylarah was 'my place to call home'. I still call it that today.

And I've always wondered, "What if my parents had kept the property?"

Meeting Pam

On December 9, 1979, I met the wonderful woman who would become my wife, and we were engaged three months later. You'll read a lot about Pam over the rest of this book – she's been my rock and has supported me over all of the phases and stages of my life.

Pam was born in Perth after her parents arrived from Bristol, England, in 1958. Her late father, John Exten, served in the British navy during the Second World War as a radar operator. He survived a frightening period of intense cold, terrifying seas and the threat from German battleships and U-boats.

He served aboard the HMS Scourge, a destroyer that escorted the Arctic convoys of merchant ships delivering essential supplies to Russia via Scotland and Iceland. Nearly 50 years later, in 1991, he was presented with the Jubilee Medal – a Russian initiative honouring those who took part in the Arctic convoys.

A great day in 1981: my wedding to Pam

Pam's mother, Barbara, worked behind the scenes during the war and lived through the Bristol Blitz – the heavy bombing of the city by the German Luftwaffe. She is 98 as I write this and lives near us in Buderim on Queensland's Sunshine Coast.

Originally, Pam wanted to be a nurse, but that didn't work out for her, so she decided to go into drafting instead. She was always very artistic, and drafting in those days was all done with pen on paper. She was also a very dedicated mother who assumed that she'd finish work for good once Yana and Jarrod were born.

However, she'd been good enough at her job that once they were grown, a previous co-worker asked her to come back and work with them. She applied, got the job and proceeded to create a career for herself in an area she's still enjoying today as I write this book.

The present-day Wylarah

Whenever I've occasionally visited Surat, I've realised that living away from the land means I've become 'soft'. I can't help but wonder whether I could have truly done justice to the property and the work required to make a living. That's how I feel now anyway – although perhaps I could have grown tougher again and been successful.

Regardless, I have overwhelming respect for farmers and people who work the land. They're not only challenged by the environment – drought, floods and fires – but also the need to diversify at different times depending on climate, economy and international trade.

My memories of Wylarah will stay with me forever. However, being sent to boarding school at Marist College in Brisbane opened up a whole new world to me. I could suddenly see what people who weren't on the land or in the bush did.

An interesting footnote to the Wylarah story is that my parents sold the property in 1976 for $25/acre. Several years later, the property was bought by an American cotton producer for $2,500/acre.

My life, from growing up on our sheep property through coaching, player welfare management, and careers in the airline, construction and education industries, has been a lesson. It's one that continues today.

Today, Wylarah is owned by AACo (Australian Agricultural Company), which specialises in grain-fed beef and Wagyu beef production. Established in 1824, AACo is Australia's largest integrated cattle and beef producer, and is the oldest continuously operating company in Australia. Quite nostalgic for the Hurst family as well.

AACo's properties, feedlots and farms comprise around 6.4 million hectares (14.8 million acres) of land in Queensland and the Northern Territory. Wylarah's purpose is breeding the renowned Westholme Wagyu herd to produce full-blood bulls for the AACo commercial herds, and feeder steers.

A recent search of Wylarah also reveals that the current manager's name is Murray. Amazing.

Billionaire Microsoft founder Bill Gates visited Wylarah in 2017 as part of his work with philanthropy organisation The Gates Foundation. When he did, he praised the breeding technologies, nutrition management, genetics knowledge and use of cutting-edge digital equipment there.

When I look back on our time at Wylarah sheep station, especially the years of hardship, and compare it to the world-renowned Wagyu stud it is today, I think: **WOW!**

A piece of verse I composed years ago...

SURAT

On the banks of the Balonne River,
Stands a little gem of a town.
In the heart of the vast Maranoa,
A jewel in a priceless crown.
The people are happy and friendly.
The way of life is sublime.
There's never a cross word to greet you,
If you stop to pass the time.
So, do yourself a favour.
Find a place to hang your hat.
And pause to smell the roses,
In the township of Surat.

CHAPTER 3

Flying High in Business and Politics

The secret of success is to be ready when opportunity comes. Don't expect opportunity to come knocking on your door. Open the door yourself.

Most people know me for my contributions to Rugby League, but my career has spanned many industries. It took me through working in the stock and station business, through a long stint with the airlines, into construction and even Catholic education, as well as politics.

But throughout the entire period, I was involved in Rugby League, either as a player or a coach. Really, some of my roles were totally unplanned. It became the norm for people to suggest a role to me and subsequently offer me a position.

More often than not, I agreed because I wanted to learn

new things and test myself. I guess this attitude exemplified the resilience that was a carry-over from my experience at Wylarah.

In each situation, my first consideration was always Pam and the children. Back when I was offered my very first A-grade coaching role, I had no idea if I'd like it or be any good at it. Now, all this time later, I believe it was a good fit with our family. Yana and Jarrod would grow up noticing the hard work I demonstrated by basically holding two jobs. Meanwhile, watching Pam working and running our home also encouraged their very obvious work ethic and resilience.

But, as I mentioned above, I've done plenty of other things besides coaching. The ability to move from one field to another and succeed in them all is a testament to how flexible and prepared growing up on the land made me.

And while Wylarah did teach me to prepare for the unknown, it also taught me to be mostly optimistic.

Taking stock

I expected a smooth transition from life on the land to my first job away from the property. I'd be working as a stock salesman for the stock and station agency Dalgety Australia Ltd in Rockhampton during 1975–1976. How wrong I was about that transition!

As the beef capital of Australia, Rockhampton was the hub for many large properties in the district. A stock salesman's job was to continually contact property owners and graziers to see whether they needed sheep or cattle sold. Salesmen needed to get the right price for the stock from a reliable buyer. More importantly, they had to establish relationships built on trust.

If the parties couldn't agree on a price per head on their own, a stock agent would facilitate the sale. Auctioneers would be present to get the highest price from bidders. People would bid on cattle and sheep per head back then, although cattle are bid on per kilogram of their weight these days.

My job as a salesman was one step on the pathway to become an auctioneer – I guess it was like a traineeship. In Rockhampton, we often attended Gracemere saleyards on Tuesdays for the weekly sales, which are still held today.

Not long after starting the job, I was lucky to survive a serious accident. I'd been to Sarina for the day to look at cattle with another Dalgety salesman and two prospective buyers. On the way back, late in the afternoon, a car pulled out to pass a truck coming the other way.

It hit us head-on.

The side of the road dropped steeply away, so we couldn't veer out of the oncoming car's path. Ironically, our vehicle finished up off the road and down the drop anyway.

I recall crawling out of the car, but not much after that. Apparently, two army trucks stopped to assist before the ambulance arrived, although by that point, I was knocked out and obviously in a bad way. The Dalgety guy with me was devastated when he saw a blanket being placed over my body and heard an army medic say, "This one's gone."

I was far from gone, but I did spend time in hospital with a broken sternum and a broken rib that had punctured my kidney. Once they'd loaded me onto the ambulance, every small bump or swerve in the road to the hospital felt like a knife going deeper into my chest. But worse than that was when the Accident & Emergency staff cut my best shirt off to determine the damage.

I was discharged a week later and spent a week or two recuperating. Soon after that, I was back at work, thankful that the army fellow's on-scene assessment had been wrong.

Up, up and away

In 1977, my career began with Trans Australia Airlines (TAA) – renamed Australian Airlines in 1986. It was an incredibly satisfying career that continued for 18 years, during which I worked in various managerial roles at North Queensland airports.

Those roles included Manager of the Mackay terminal and city office, Terminal Supervisor at Townsville, and Passenger Services Supervisor at Rockhampton. I also held the role of Traffic Manager role in Townsville and Mackay with responsibility for passenger check-in, aircraft load control and aircraft marshalling. The latter role involved standing on the tarmac and using baton signals to direct the pilot to the terminal parking spot.

At one point, I was also Manager of Executive Travel in Brisbane.

One newspaper journalist got completely carried away and stated in an article that I was an air traffic controller. He mentioned that this job required planning, logic and calm, then said I'd applied those attributes to my coaching career! He obviously mistook my role as the airport's 'Traffic Manager' as instead being 'Air Traffic Controller' – the job that entails directing aircraft safely through airspace and into and out of airports.

I'll also never forget my time at Townsville Airport, which had an old terminal that was constructed of timber and tin. The staff culture involved a lot of drinking and partying, which was a real eye-opener to me. Each day, people would finish their shift and gather at the airport bar. Some would even finish a night shift, sleep in the terminal, then go back to the TAA counter for the early morning shift the next day.

Occasionally, this would result in some dangerous situations. One Christmas Day, we needed to load a female passenger in a wheelchair into an aircraft using a forklift. The forklift driver was visibly under the influence and accidentally tilted the tray forward, which nearly caused the passenger's wheelchair to topple off. If I hadn't been on the tray with her, she'd have fallen onto the tarmac and potentially been seriously injured.

Luckily, workplace health and safety protocols have changed markedly since those days – even the name has now changed to occupational health and safety.

I think that was around the same time that I was standing on the tarmac and marshalling a Boeing 747 aircraft in 46-degree heat. I moved to plug the headset into the aircraft to speak with the skipper and somehow accidentally stepped out of my shoes, which stayed in the tar. It was funny, but not much fun.

On another occasion, I was checking in a passenger when a cat suddenly fell from a manhole in the ceiling onto my seat-allocation chart. The startled passenger and I looked at each other, the feisty feline sped off, and we carried on.

And on yet another day, I arrived at 5am for my shift and had to pick up a very well-known Australian actor from the gutter outside the terminal. A strong smell of alcohol hung in the air. He was a little different then to the characters he's portrayed in movies!

Hiatus at Peak Downs mine

In 1985, Pam, Yana, Jarrod and I had an interesting and unforgettable experience when I had an eight-month hiatus from the airline industry. I decided to instead take up a role as a laboratory assistant at Peak Downs coal mine in Central Queensland.

During that time, we lived in Moranbah, which is two and a half hours west of Mackay. My brother, Hilton, who worked in the mining industry, told me about the laboratory assistant position at the mine. This role involved testing different stages and levels of coal preparation and quality.

I'd just been appointed Terminal Supervisor at Townsville Airport when I heard I'd also got the job in the mine. I needed to make a decision. Did I take more money in the mine to better my family? Or did I accept the role in the airline and a prospective long-term career?

This is the only time I shouldn't have taken Dad's advice. He thought it was better to have a role where you can go to work, do your eight hours and come home with no thought of your job. So off we went to Moranbah.

However, I quickly discovered that collecting samples in a wash-plant and routinely testing them wasn't for me. It was then I realised that I'd prefer to be in charge of people rather than fit in and be told what to do.

During that period, we had an incident as a family that we were lucky to walk away from. We'd spent the Christmas break in Rockhampton, visiting both of our parents. The four-hour drive back was going smoothly when a tyre blew out near a small town called Tieri.

The car fishtailed then rolled twice before settling upside-down across a gully on the right-hand side of the Peak Downs Highway. The moment we landed, my first thought was to get everyone out of the car. So I pressed the seatbelt release buttons and the children fell to the roof. Yana was three years old and Jarrod was just six months at the time. Another of my vivid memories is that the first thing Yana said when she stood up was, "Are you alright, Dad?"

We hadn't long been out of the car when a tow truck pulled up beside us. The driver called his wife, who collected Pam and the children, took them to their home in Tieri and gave them something to eat. Meanwhile, I helped him load the car and take it to the police station.

I blame myself for the accident, as I may have braked when I heard the tyre blow out. We were so very lucky – the consequences could have been so much worse. Thank the Lord, everyone came through well apart from a piece of glass lodging in Pam's elbow.

However, the accident tipped us over the edge of a decision we'd already been considering after Yana developed an asthmatic condition from the coal dust in the Moranbah region. Well, that plus the fact that, shortly afterwards, the Manager of Australian Airlines in Townsville called me to see if I was happy in the mining industry. Apparently, there was a role available at the airport for me if I wanted it.

So after an eight-month hiatus that could be preceded by the adjective 'regrettable', we moved back to Townsville again!

Murray the politician?

Although I'd always had an interest in the big picture of politics, I never thought I'd see the day I'd become a politician. In 2004, however, I was encouraged to run for local government due to the community support I'd received during my coaching stint with the Cowboys. It was support that only increased after I left the club.

I ran for office in Thuringowa – a sister city to Townsville – and was elected to the Thuringowa City Council for a four-year term as a councillor. I always believed, and still do, that local government should be apolitical. This level is where you can simply help people. There's a more face-to-face aspect to the role without playing politics. My jurisdictions included Corporate Governance, Business Units, Australian Crime Prevention Council, Urban Design, and Commercial and Economic Development.

I must have done a reasonable job because two sitting mayors – Les Tyrell (Thuringowa) and Tony Mooney (Townsville) – asked me to run as their deputy mayor. That was in the 2008 Townsville City Council election, the first for the amalgamated Townsville Regional Council. The political machinations were too much for me, however. So I declined both offers, not wishing to offend anyone.

The next year, though, the Liberal National Party (LNP) persuaded me to run for them in the 2009 state election. They wanted to secure the seat of Townsville, which was a Labor stronghold at the time. Australian and Queensland State of Origin great Shane Webcke – whom I knew from the 2001 State of Origin campaign – endorsed me for the election. His picture even appeared on my campaign advertising flyers. John Doyle and Matt Bowen also endorsed me.

It wasn't to be though. In the final wash-up, I ended up short in the primary count by 1,268 votes. I did, however, secure a swing of 5.4% to the LNP.

It was probably for the best. While I enjoyed my time in local government, I wasn't keen on the party politics of state government. Yes, I was disappointed I didn't win the seat of Townsville: I would have liked to work with LNP leader Lawrence Springborg, whom I had a lot of respect for. But at the same time, I also felt a great sense of relief that my days as a politician were at an end.

I believe there are too many levels of government in Australia. We only need federal and local governments.

Management roles across sectors

I was also privileged to work for Townsville Catholic Education from 2005 to 2008 as Facilities Planning and Development Manager. I led the process of applying for state and federal government grants to construct new schools and extensions throughout the Townsville diocese. This area encompassed more than 30 primary and secondary schools.

My role involved consulting with school principals, parish priests, parent groups, education consultants, members of other church agencies, and government departments and architects. It was complex, but I found it extremely rewarding to see successfully completed projects.

The environment at Townsville Catholic Education was very much aligned with what I stood for. In particular, I discovered that the prayer sessions and meditations were of great benefit as I tried to heal the scars after my demise with the Cowboys. I was also surprised at just how many people I knew in the Catholic system and the empathy they showed.

I left the organisation early in 2008 but returned a year later as New Projects Manager. I remained there until April 2012 when I joined the NRL.

The year I spent away from Townsville Catholic Education was due to a job offer I received out of the blue. Apparently, Beckside Constructions and Abec Homes in Mackay needed a General Manager. The salary, along with the opportunity to coach the Brothers team in Mackay, seemed attractive. Pam was also keen to return to Mackay after the enjoyable two years we'd spent there in 1989 and 1990. She secured a job as a civil designer with the multinational engineering firm AECOM.

While my coaching stint at Brothers was successful, the reverse unfolded at Beckside Constructions when the company got into dire straits financially. I felt embarrassed that I hadn't done my due diligence before taking on the role as General Manager after realising that the company had run up substantial debt before my arrival.

As the year progressed, the company's collapse seemed inevitable, so Pam and I decided to return to Townsville.

My curriculum vitae shows that I squeezed in several other interesting jobs during the 2000s too. One was with the Townsville Toyota dealer selling Lexus cars. I even featured in a television advertisement as 'Mr Lexus'. Amazingly, it worked – I won the Australian Regional Lexus Salesperson of the Year award!

To this day, I can't recall selling anything. This wasn't long after my demise at the Cowboys, so I don't think my state of mind was great. In fact, I can't remember a lot of what happened in the 12 months afterwards.

However, one thing I'll never forget from my time with the dealer was when a casually dressed guy came into the showroom to look at a Toyota ute. None of the sales staff paid any attention to him, assuming he wouldn't buy anything. Later, we learnt that he'd gone straight to another dealer and bought 57 utes from them.

Lesson: Don't judge a book by its cover. Never assume!

Another job I had in Townsville was as Manager of the Carlyle Gardens Lifestyle Village, which had 386 homes and 500 residents. This was an over-50s community, and I enjoyed interacting with the residents and managing the construction of 20 new homes.

On one occasion when I was signing a new couple into the village, I advised them that the lease period was 99 years. The gentleman asked me, "What happens at the end of the lease?"

I replied, "I don't think you need to worry about that." His wife saw the funny side, thankfully.

> *My work in each of these fields has taught me different skills, especially people skills, as well as created new understandings that have formed my philosophies in life.*

We all have experiences during our employment years that serve as good and bad memories, and therefore stories to tell. I'm aware that sometimes, these stories may only be of interest to family and certain friends, so I have purposely not ventured that way. However, I'm pleased and proud that I've delved into so many lines of employment. I can't imagine completing my entire work life within one organisation or industry – unless, of course, I'd remained on the land at Wylarah.

Meeting new people is very good for your growth and soul. Through all my roles, a few common values or traits have emerged: helping people, loyalty, empathy and certainly resilience. I know this versatility and success would never have come my way had I not met Pam, which couldn't have happened if I'd stayed on the property. Changing jobs and places of residence is not for everyone, but it seems to have been ideal for me and my family.

So if your employment path has been difficult, I hope you get the message that there's no shame in changing jobs. The important thing is to give your best to the opportunities that present themselves. Be ready to listen, and be ready to learn.

I'll go further into my Rugby League coaching career next, as I know that's what most people want to read about. I'll tell you about my coaching philosophy and the importance of mental toughness, solid values and being a team player in the next chapter.

CHAPTER 4

Coaching – Where it Began

Bring your best to be your best. Each and every time you train, each and every time you play, be sure to give your absolute best.

My coaching career started in Townsville in 1988 with a role that was completely out of left field: coaching the Brothers A-grade team. At the time, the Brothers had clubs in several towns, including both Townsville and Mackay.

Jarrod and Yana were aged three and six back then, and I was working shifts at the airline. Pam hadn't planned to work while the children were young, and coaching meant extra income to support our family. On the other hand, it also meant more time away from the children for me. Plus, to ensure I could be at all three weekly training sessions and every game, I needed to swap some shifts with co-workers. Luckily, they were very accepting of my predicament: something I haven't forgotten.

NORTH ROCKHAMPTON FOOTBALL CLUB
"A" GRADE GRAND PREMIERS 1980

Back Row : — J. MILNE (Manager), R. LORRAWAY, M. GOODE, T. ALDRED, T. BARRETT, M. HURST, S. WEBBER (Trainer).
Middle Row : — J. BROWNING (Treasurer), K. YEWDALE, K. PARSONS, K. KERR, R. KERR, J. LIDDELL, D. NEWMAN, M. GRIFFIN (Secretary).
Front Row : — C. ROTHERY, W. SEAR, W. ROWLAND (Coach), T. GOODE (Captain), J. MINTO (President), M. TANSWELL, M. HORSTMAN.
Absent : — G. CHALMERS, J. NEWSOME.
— (LAUREEN STUDIOS)

During my playing days: Rockhampton Premiers 1980

I still feel today that this level of coaching is the most satisfying and enjoyable in many ways. Players just love the game and want to be with their mates, and most of them aspired to greater heights in the game.

Before coaching the Brothers, I'd played A-grade Rugby League for 10 years in both Rockhampton and Townsville. I'd also played A-grade Rugby Union for three years in both cities. And in both codes, I played at five-eighth.

I definitely enjoyed my time in Rugby Union. Not only was I part of three premiership-winning teams, but I also loved the camaraderie within the teams and the post-match socialising with the opposition. In those days, the player dynamic between the two codes was quite different.

In Rugby Union, simply clapping the opposition off the field was heartening. It was like the adage 'what happens on the field stays on the field, and let's have a beer together afterwards', which is what used to happen. This occurred at both a club and representative level. The unmarried Rugby Union boys would play drinking games afterwards. Meanwhile, the League players stuck with their own club-mates when they had a drink.

The contrast between playing at this level and playing full-time professional Rugby League is marked. The A-grade level is where most players begin their football. They play to be with their mates and to enjoy the game. Only then do they feel a yearning to reach the heights where the competition is very strong. They normally discover this after they're selected to be in representative teams – someone notices them and the big clubs come knocking.

Some players prefer to continue at the amateur level. It provides an outlet from their jobs, and I now realise that it's also good for their mental health. They can enjoy playing more when their livelihoods aren't in danger from a string of poor performances. Personally, though, I liked to play against the best. At least it let me discover whether I was capable of advancing.

It may sound arrogant, but I played League for many years without a coach ever teaching me anything. I just learnt by playing with and watching good players. Mind you, a particularly good Rugby Union coach in Rockhampton, Terry Carew, taught me a lot about teamwork and game sense. So it wasn't that I didn't want to learn.

During my final couple of seasons playing Rugby League with the Townsville Brothers, the club administration noticed that I might be suited to coaching. My teammates often came to me to ask my opinion on their performance and what I thought they needed to do better. Club president Gavin Lyons must have noticed what was happening because the next year I was somehow coaching the A-grade side. I hadn't expected or planned to do this – I even suggested they should look elsewhere – but I took it on because the club wanted me to.

Another highlight of my time playing Rugby Union was representing Queensland Country against Brisbane. We played at that great Rugby ground Ballymore, which is a world-renowned arena for Brisbane club, state and international Rugby. There's so much history associated with the ground due to the success of various Queensland representative teams over the decades. And some of the all-time greats were part of it all too.

Coaching – Where it Began

One of 90 goals I kicked in 1983

Australia has had enormous success at Ballymore as well. There was only ever a grandstand on the western side. Meanwhile, the 'hills' on the three other sides would get packed with spectators, which made for a great atmosphere. When the game was amateur, the ground was the headquarters of Rugby Union – not just in Queensland, but throughout Australia. Sadly, the Queensland Rugby Union (QRU) administration couldn't secure funding to upgrade the arena, so games moved to Suncorp Stadium.

As I write, Ballymore has been closed and is being completely redeveloped.

The importance of values

When I started coaching in 1988, my initial aim was to ensure that all players got on, were happy and supported one another without agendas. To make this happen, I insisted on players looking me in the eye when I spoke with them, both individually and as a group. My father instilled this in me, and I've passed it on to Jarrod.

Meeting someone's eye may not seem much to some people, but I believe it's a sign of genuineness and legitimacy.

Funnily enough, I never really wanted to coach. I strongly believe that players learn more about the game in their final playing year or after they retire than they did from their early career coaches. At this point, they can watch the game and analyse it from a different perspective in terms of how players react to possession and field positioning.

> *Each year as a coach, I aimed to improve the players – not only as footballers but also as people.*

I believe I consistently achieved that throughout my career.

Even in my first year at the Cowboys, I found it easy to relate to state and national players. This trait was probably born from my beliefs around the first meeting – looking people in the eye – as well as my honesty. I earned respect from these players rather than demanded it.

Coaching Rugby League requires 80% people skills. The rest is made up of a good knowledge of the game, and the ability to design and coach skills for players. Skills coaching was a strong suit of mine, although not by planning – I never sat down and decided what I wanted to be good at. Rather, from the beginning, I seemed to possess an innate ability to detect both individual and team skills. I could see what skill each player required to succeed, and then could devise drills and activities to enhance that skill.

However, that doesn't mean I didn't plan. There's no point attempting a task without a clear vision, and that means developing a flawless overall plan. Creating success in sport or business requires an effective, solid administration with a strong strategy. That, in turn, translates to a good culture. In Rugby League, the vital ingredient is 'positive team culture', which is driven by the coach.

That means coaches are the essence of planning, perseverance and total commitment.

Achievements also take complete commitment and dedication. As a coach, you set the process in place for the entire week, devising a plan to combat the opposition's attack and exploit their weaknesses.

Two players I relied on heavily to 'run this plan' at the Cowboys were Noel Goldthorpe and Scott Prince. They were both halfbacks who were like coaches on the field. They understood every player's role and directed them accordingly. Then, up front, were the 'foot soldiers' – tough men like Ian Roberts, John Buttigieg and Tim Maddison to name just a few. They were critical to the game plan in providing the go-forward on the field.

Toughness between the ears

Mental toughness is vital for all top-level athletes, and it can either be learnt or inherited. Players can learn it by way of consistent, extremely tough training, where each and every session requires 100% effort to the extent that the athlete just can't give anymore.

This can take months, if not years.

Inherited mental toughness is often a result of a person's

socio-economic background together with their upbringing. I've always believed that country people have enormous mental toughness and resilience. They're normally positive and realistic, calm and relaxed under fire, highly energetic and doggedly determined.

Mental toughness can make all the difference. On one hand, a team can have the skills, fitness and speed to win any game, but can't – as a group – persevere when things go against them. Compare this team with one that lacks some of the physical traits mentioned but hangs in there, staying in each moment and nailing opportunities that present themselves. The latter team takes advantage of the big moments. Players who are already mentally tough require much less development in this area, and the other players will learn from them.

The best example of the two spectrums is in State of Origin, comparing Queensland to NSW. Queensland achieved eight successive State of Origin series victories, and most of their players had a country background. Meanwhile, I have no idea about the NSW team's makeup, but when the crunch came and the games were in balance, Queensland would usually reign supreme.

I don't think it's possible for a player to be a champion until they've played a minimum of ten years at the top level. I believe the word 'champion' is used too loosely... and 'great' even more so. I also believe that Rugby League is the toughest collision sport in the world. I say this comparing it to GridIron (NFL),

Rugby Union and Australian Rules. Collisions are much more frequent in Rugby League.

Here's my rationale around calling players 'champions'. The average career of a top-level League player ten years ago was 42 games. Now it's 59 games – partly as a result of the convention of player 'interchange' (where some players don't spend the full 80 minutes on the field). With around 24 games each year, this equates to an average career of two years ten years ago, and three years now.

In other words, the career window is very small.

Ten years ago, people who reached the 200-game mark were extraordinary, but nowadays, it's very common. This is due to faster games today along with greater fitness, athleticism and smarts. Today, many people have reached the 300-game milestone, but only one ever reached over 400: the incredible Cameron Smith. I believe players who reached 300 games are 'greats', while Cameron is the greatest (if not the smartest).

The reason I say this is that in each year they play, a player understands more about the game, themselves and their role within the team. This means anxiety becomes less of an issue for their performance, and they stop beating themselves up after a loss. Instead, they learn from it and encourage teammates to do the same.

My coaching methods and philosophies were based around quite uncomplicated triggers.

In addition to mental toughness, discipline at training and on game day is paramount at all levels. Discipline means sticking to routines, holding your anger in check and not reacting when provoked or distracted. It also means being diligent with every task you take on. It means not passing if there's any doubt that the ball may go to ground. And it means doing your job until the final whistle without blame.

From the beginning, I also saw coaching as requiring strict discipline around punctuality. This had to start with me. The players needed to recognise my commitment and duplicate the standards I set. Players always watch the coach, and most of the time they listen as well. If training began at 6pm, I expected players to be there by 5.45pm. That meant I needed to be there no later than 5.30pm.

If a player arrived at 6pm, I barred them from playing in the coming match.

Some coaches have great ideas about how they want their team to play but have trouble explaining their game plan and processes. They also have difficulty explaining the reason for the training drill they've set out on the field. It isn't coaching to simply get satisfaction from watching players running around marker-domes, passing the ball left and right, and hearing voices calling for the ball. You must be able to explain the reasons for doing each drill and show players how they'll incorporate it into the match plan.

The modern game has assistant coaches who focus specifically on this task.

The long sessions I put players through early in my coaching career were a lesson in more ways than one. Obviously, I wanted perfection in whatever I asked the players to perform. But it was also a process that served as a lesson in life. They needed total commitment to their task to the extent that it takes time to get it right, along with perseverance and concentration.

My theory is that learning a new skill requires carrying out a drill up to 100 times. You can reduce this number if you have a player or two who already has the skill in their repertoire. This means that the other players can watch them demonstrate it and then replicate it.

I guess this repetition at training contributed to what I was well known for: long training sessions of up to three hours. This was even at a grassroots level. I recall one year when the players arrived at training each with a sleeping bag. I loved it, but I had to buy them breakfast!

One thing I've always believed is that players don't complain if you keep them winning. And over the years, I coached many players who improved enough to become Queensland and Australian representatives. As other coaches who've done this would say, those players don't forget where they came from.

There are always exceptions, of course, but I don't resent them for forgetting – that's not the reason anyone should coach. Self-satisfaction is more important than acknowledgement: after all, you have your career and they have theirs.

*I earned respect from these players,
but I never demanded it.*

> Some of the coaching key points that proved successful for me were:
>
> - I never judge a player's skill level based solely on one or two training sessions, just like I don't judge a person on first introduction.
> - Every player has a trait or skill that is their strength, so devise a method to let them use it in games for the benefit of the team.
> - Identify your leader or leaders as early as possible. Listen and watch them very closely. Notice the reaction from their peers. This is most important in representative teams.
> - You can create leaders.
> - Identify one or two players who have the

'big picture' of the game and the field in their mind. These are your pivotal players – the 'ball-players' who run the game. The remaining players 'run' and only need to be able to tip-on. Power-running is essential.

- Run to run. This means always intending to run *through* the defensive line, not just *to* it. Also, don't run to get tackled.

- One ball-player can suffice, but it's ideal to have two or three – ie. the two halves and hooker. These days there can even be four with the fullback ball-playing.

- Off-the-ground speed and defence-line speed take up 60% of my training sessions, including 'shoulders in tackles'. At one club, we won six premierships with a mantra of SOG and SOL – Speed Off the Ground and Speed Off the Line. This is how Rugby League speeds up.

- After a tackle, aim to achieve your defensive position in the line before the ball has been played.

- All tackles are everyone's responsibility. That is, even if you're not involved in a

> tackle, you're responsible for the ensuing play.
>
> - There's no point in having a plan in mind of how you want your team to play if you don't have the players to enact that plan. A plan that's too complicated will also prove fruitless.
>
> - If you have a naturally instinctive player, be very careful not to give them too much structure. Let them play it how they see it.
>
> - All passes must be in front of the receiver – BIF (Ball in Front).

I mention in the above points that a leader can be created, although many coaches wouldn't agree with this. Identifying a player who sees the 'big picture' on the field and commands respect off it is another challenge that some coaches handle well while others don't.

A skipper doesn't simply have a 'c' next to their name and run out first. They're the most important person for the group's dynamic and the respect that is given. Most of the teams with long runs of winning are captained by a player who commands respect on and off the field. Teammates look to them for guidance on how to act and react. I've had a representative team gather and the squad comprised the four players who captained their club.

The skill of listening is the greatest skill of all.

I recommend choosing who will lead such a group throughout the few days you spend together. Watch, listen and learn as much as you can from each candidate and see how other members react to them. You don't necessarily need to choose an 'elder statesman' for your club skipper. I prefer someone who is a good person and leads by example in all ways.

Coaching players from other cultures, in my case Tongan, is quite a different situation altogether. In fact, it's so different that it deserves its own chapter. So read on for those stories.

CHAPTER 5

Taking Tonga to the World Cup

Winning is a process that requires a solid foundation with a good beginning.

I was appointed national coach of Tonga in 1998 as a lead-in to the 2000 World Cup. At the time, I was employed by the Cowboys, which meant that they were my priority. Additionally, while I spent three or four weeks in Nuku'alofa in 1998, and again in 1999, my family stayed in Townsville as the children were still in school.

And although we never made it to the quarter-finals of the World Cup in 2000, Tonga's potential to become an exciting force in test Rugby League was evident.

At the time, Tongans seemed to hold a long-lived belief that their players were somewhat inferior to those who played in Australia and England. This was probably born from their admiration of the players they'd seen on television over time.

But if they witnessed a fellow Tongan player matching it with the best, the whole country would be in raptures. And when the Tongan players had the chance to compete against world-class international players, the Tongan people as a whole held them in awe.

However, the belief in Tongan player inferiority might have been the result of a mental toughness issue – something I needed to discover. Players were certainly physically more than equal, so perhaps it was skill or aerobic capacity. Regardless, the Tongan players always looked imposing at first sight to their opposition at game kick-offs. And opposition teams can't always get over this view of them, making the Tongan team very tough to defeat.

Tonga finally saw their first success at the 2017 World Cup when they beat New Zealand 28–22 to clinch a semi-final berth. Although I wasn't the coach at the time, I was very pleased for them. It was the first time a tier-two nation had beaten a tier-one team at a World Cup. Eventually, Tonga lost the semi-final to England 20–18. However, in 2019, they shocked Rugby League to its core when they beat world champions Australia 16–12 in the Oceania Cup.

Preparing for the future

Back in 1998, my first job as coach for Tonga was to travel to the kingdom to assess the standard of players and competition. The respect that the players and the Tonga National Rugby League board, in particular the president Viliame Fukofuka, afforded me was a delight.

I could call training with different squads at any time of day and receive nothing less than 100% effort and commitment. Player skills required a lot of attention, and I needed to lower my expectations. At that point, I'd been with the Cowboys for three years. Cowboys players were all full-time professionals who'd had a lot of skills training over many seasons, firstly as juniors and then at senior level. The Tongans were all amateur players so they needed time.

It was satisfying, after players and staff put in the work, to see their skills and understanding of the game improve rapidly. However, one aspect that concerned me was the players' aerobic fitness, which determined their ability to play the full 80 minutes. As I've said previously, getting off the ground quickly after making tackles and achieving the defensive line is the toughest part of the game.

Players were all fast and explosive, but lasting the distance seemed to be a problem. Also, back then there was no player interchange – when players can 'rest' during a game – as there is now. Today, interchange means that when a player appears to be 'gassed', a fresh player can replace them. They can then be injected back into the game at a later time. In 1998, however, this wasn't an option. So players' aerobic fitness required work to ensure they could play for longer periods.

I went to Tonga again in 1999 to prepare the Mate Ma'a

team for a tour to the Cook Islands for three tests. Incidentally, Mate Ma'a Tonga means 'die for Tonga'. All the Tongans I met epitomised this mantra, showing it through their passion and their performance of their haka, the Sipi Tau. It was a joy to return to the people involved, the players and the country itself.

Your mind is like an umbrella. It won't work properly if it isn't open.

—adapted from Henry Ford

For the first week, I trained the squad every day, taking time off only for meals. Not a single player complained during this time. In fact, with the support of the captain, Lani Filiai, players couldn't get enough of my training. This was so different to some of the full-time professional players I'd become used to.

Lani could speak reasonable English, so he also interpreted my instructions for the other players, as well as encouraging each player and the team overall. Even though I didn't speak Tongan at the beginning, I could see that the players' body language was always positive. And whenever Lani sensed that I was pushing them too hard, he would give me feedback, which worked well. I learnt quite a bit of the language while I was there too.

Unfortunately, for a county-raised man like me, Tongan names were hard to pronounce initially. For example, there were players such as Tu'ihakavalu Afungia, Simi Fakavoemianga, Leho Lutunipulu, Simione Foliaki, Tevita Kaufusi and Alafaki.

However, as time passed and I needed to nominate players in different drills, I needed to learn to say their names properly. For a while, I found it helped to think of the names as merely sounds and then they seemed to roll off my tongue easily. Eventually, I didn't even have to think about them.

Sometimes, the players would tease me. As an example, when I met Alafaki, a well-educated man with a cheeky sense of humour, he said, "You can call me Faki." He pronounced his name much like the English swear word, effectively daring me to say it that way for the entire time I was there.

I looked him right in the eye, letting him know I'd caught the joke, and said, "No, I'll call you Ala."

He just laughed, not at all put out at having been caught.

Lunch was always an interesting break as things seemed to occur that I could never have predicted or expected. Close to the break on one occasion, I wondered what they'd eat for lunch. Then a truck arrived. The players jumped up into the truck, sat on benches inside it and awaited instruction to begin eating.

Near the back of the truck were 20 unsliced loaves of bread and a cut-off 44-gallon drum. The drum was full of a grain-and-water porridge, which had obviously been cooked a lot earlier that day as there was a thick crust on it. The players broke the bread up with their hands, then dipped their piece into the porridge to scoop it up. The break lasted 15 minutes, but they ate heartily. In fact, one of the props, Nuku, had eaten so much so quickly that his stomach was visibly swollen. He just lay on the ground on his back for some time, unable to train that afternoon.

During another lunch break, I noticed that the halfback Samuela Fukofuka was absent. Enquiring about his whereabouts yielded a simple shrug from the players. We began the afternoon session without him, but eventually, I noticed him appear during a drink break.

I asked him where he'd been, and he replied, "I, uh, I got married," while looking down the front of his pants. I saw this as a clear sign that he'd also consummated the marriage. Lani later told me that Sammy had arranged the service and feast for a time that he'd hoped wouldn't interfere with his training. Unfortunately for him, the timing had clashed, so he'd done his best to resolve the 'double booking'.

And to my knowledge, Lani was the only player aware that Sammy was getting married that day.

The journey to the Cook Islands

The players were excited when the time came to depart Tonga's capital Nuku'alofa as a squad for the Cook Islands tour. In fact, I'd never seen such excitement. Small crop farming and fishing were the main industries of Tonga at that time, along with some tourism. This meant most players hadn't travelled out of Tonga before, although some had been to Auckland – either with family or for higher education. None of them had been to the Cook Islands, though. That meant they weren't aware

With Tonga at the Cook Islands in 1999

of customs procedures, and our team manager Molakai had to school them on these.

Our accommodation in the Cook Islands capital, Rarotonga, was in a motel that roomed the players in pairs. I was humbled by the respect they showed me while I was there. At mealtime, they wouldn't sit at the table until I sat down or begin eating until I did. Many were also unfamiliar with Western breakfast foods. At home in Tonga, they'd normally eat taro, porridge or bread and pork for breakfast. None of them had ever come across cornflakes before.

It didn't even occur to me to tell them that we'd normally add milk to cornflakes – that was just something I'd always taken for granted. So I was surprised to see that, one morning when the motel owners brought out cornflakes for breakfast, the players poured orange juice on them. Then, not wanting to waste the milk on the table, they drank that.

It was a good lesson for me in avoiding assumptions!

We gave the players $5 a day for expenses, but some of them weren't used to money. The first morning of recreation time they had, every one of them purchased a $15 wallet. They had nothing to put into the wallets, but they had to have them nonetheless.

For each training session, we travelled by bus to the national sporting ground. I'll never forget how the Tongan players sang on the ride during every journey. From origin to destination, they'd make the bus reverberate in perfect harmony. Apart from some walks together as a squad, we were always on that bus.

The incredible thing with their harmonious singing was that they'd never pre-determine or pre-arrange the music. They'd just file onto the bus, sit anywhere and start singing as soon as we set off. Every player sang, and everyone knew every word of so many traditional songs. I even found myself singing with them a few times. They also entertained the patrons at our accommodation after dinner one night.

Time for the tests

The three tests we would play were controlled by NRL referee Brian Grant. I didn't know how the team would perform against opposition: a group can quite often look fast and slick at training, yet get into a collision situation against opposition and fall apart. I needn't have worried, however, as our group absolutely loved the contact and collision in the first test.

Better yet, the team continually forced errors and had most of the possession. This eventuated in a 40-point win for us. The singing continued on the return trip from the stadium to the motel with the same tempo as it had on the way there. The players impressed me with the way they always seemed so grateful for anything they had.

The second test was a much tougher affair. We gained control of the match early in the second half when the Cook Islanders' enthusiasm faded. Even so, we won by a narrower margin of 14 points.

Brian mentioned to me later that he'd never seen a player as quick as our centre Tevita Pole'o. I agreed that he was one of the quickest humans playing Rugby League. He was one of the rare athletes who commanded attention – whenever he was in full flight, he made everyone else look like they were standing still. I think he scored eight or nine tries over the three tests.

I had to ask myself what could have eventuated if Tevita had been coached in athletics.

Our final test was three days later, and we knew there'd be an all-out attack to salvage the Cook Islanders' pride. This meant that rest, by way of stretching sessions and walks for the players, was paramount.

Knowing this, I was nervous, but our squad gelled very well in the two weeks we were in Rarotonga, and the third test saw our biggest win. I was so pleased – both for the players and for Tonga as a country. The singing, praying and presentation – both before and after the matches – seemed louder than the previous two tests.

After each game, the players would gather in a room where they'd pray and continue singing in marvellous harmony. I looked forward to this so much. During this gathering, I would nominate a 'player of the match' and present him with a jersey. After this match, I awarded the title to Tevita Kaufusi, our fullback, and tears flowed down his bare chest as he thanked me, his teammates and Tonga. His tears made the occasion very emotional for me as well.

*When a player says, "I love you, Murray,"
it's hard not to become emotional.*

After the third test, we all needed to board a flight early the next morning to Auckland. I advised the players that when we got there, they'd get on a flight to Nuku'alofa and I'd board a different flight to Sydney and then Townsville.

When we arrived in Auckland, I explained to them again that we'd board different flights to our respective homes. I didn't realise that the Tongan custom of respect and saying goodbye is to clasp hands as though you're going to shake hands, and then touch right cheek to right cheek. The first player started to grab my hand, but then just grabbed me and hugged me instead. His tears settled on my right shoulder. The remaining 21 players repeated this exactly. As the last player hugged me, my right sleeve was saturated with tears.

Leaving these dedicated, delightful people was hard, and we were all emotional. This memory will remain with me forever.

Later, in September 2000, the New Zealand Rugby League invited Tonga to play a test against the Kiwis at Carlaw Park in Auckland. The game was sanctioned by the international body and would be a good trial for the World Cup in England and France in October.

I selected a group of the Tongan resident players who'd impressed me during the Cook Islands tour. They would then join an equal number of Tongan players from the higher competitions in Australia and New Zealand to form a strong squad.

I couldn't select current Tongan NRL players, however, as their clubs wouldn't release them for a trial – which is their right as the players' employers. I saw this test as an opportunity to see how the players would perform against world-class professional Rugby League players across the board. And all I can say looking back is, "Tonga v NZ. Wow."

During the game, the Kiwis dominated possession to the tune of 80% and scored several well-structured tries. Meanwhile, my group struggled with the tough part – namely, getting off the ground and quickly achieving defensive positions. The fitness levels were a contrast.

As a result, there was a 50-point gap in the final score line. However, the exercise wasn't futile: I had a good gauge of several individuals under consideration for the World Cup.

And for that team, I'd also be able to select Tongan players from the NRL and English Super League.

The big stage: the World Cup

In the lead-up to the October 2000 World Cup, the team and I would stay in Perpignan in the south of France for three weeks. There was no shortage of players wanting to make themselves available for selection, but I knew I needed to carefully choose the squad. I had to consider not just each player's reputation and name, but also their personality, skill and whether they'd fit the team dynamic.

One such player was John Hopoate, who was on a three-game suspension for foul play. He suggested that he could come on the tour and serve his suspension through the pool games, then just play finals. Sorry, John, but no! To be fair, I found him a really nice person to chat to and his experience may have benefited the squad, but I needed to be more strategic.

In the end, we had several top-level players in our group, including Tevita Vaikona, Martin Masella, Brent Kite, Willie Mason, Andrew Lomu, Phil Howlett and Duane Mann.

Playing the South African Rhinos at Le Parc des Princes

stadium in Paris was a tremendous experience in itself. However, pulling off a 50-point win made the trip back to Perpignan something to savour. I'd made Tevita Vaikona captain of Tonga for the World Cup. As a centre, he led the team well during the game and was rightfully awarded best-on-ground. Willie Mason and Andrew Lomu both proved too strong for the South Africans, and Phil Howlett excelled at five-eighth, a position he hadn't played previously.

In our next encounter, we came up against a very committed France at Carcassonne. Examining the field, I was surprised at the depth of the in-goal area at both ends. They were 15 metres in depth, far beyond the mandatory range of 6–11 metres. When rorting such as this occurs, the home team usually carries it out for a specific reason. Sure enough, the Frenchmen had a very good short kicking game and came up with three tries from very deft kicks.

Meanwhile, the Tongan forwards were very physical against the French – and they needed to be. The opposition forwards were not only tough to handle, but they also received somewhat of a leg-up from the referee, who happened to be French. In fact, the spite began early in the game and we didn't back down from it.

I recall vividly illegal work from the French players going into tackles and the referee taking no action. I didn't say anything at the time because I thought it was probably the result of different referee interpretations of rules. Regardless, I didn't want to start a fire by complaining.

However, when the Tongan team reciprocated these tactics, it proved detrimental: we were penalised to the tune of 21–4. Then, despite winning the match 28–8, the French were inhospitable at the post-match function. Over time, I've come to believe that the French often resorted to unfamiliar tactics to unsettle the teams they play against. Then, when these tactics succeed, they see no reason to socialise with those teams. Our players had their heads down and probably would have preferred to stay with their own as well.

Our final pool game was against the Papua New Guinea Kumuls in Perpignan, which we needed to win to reach the quarter-finals. We had a strong, well-drilled side for the game. However, the Kumuls were captained by Adrian Lam, who'd played close to 150 games for the Sydney Roosters and been coached by Bob Bennett, Wayne's brother. Having won their previous two games against France and South Africa, they were the surprise packet of the 2000 World Cup.

The Kumuls edged us out by eight points, and watching Adrian Lam's orchestration in directing his team was something to behold. His experience was something we simply couldn't combat. It was as though he played in a dinner suit – we couldn't get to him.

Despite this, however, we had some very good performers in our group, especially Tevita Vaikona. He was selected in the

2000 World Cup 'Team of the Tournament' from three games, which was nothing short of extraordinary. This team was a selection of the best players across all the teams entered, for each position. At the end of the tournament, this created a list of the top performer for each position. If all these players played together, they'd make up the 'super team' from those who played in that year's matches.

Tevita's selection was even more extraordinary given that 16 countries were involved in the World Cup and 31 games were played. All other selected players came from teams that played well into the semi-finals.

Surprise coaching offers from the French

While I was in France for the World Cup, I was called to a meeting with the heads of the Catalan and French Rugby League organisations. They told me they had plans to enter a French team in the English Super League in the next few years and wanted to sound me out as a coaching candidate.

While I loved the south of France, I thought their plan was somewhat ambitious. However, I did show interest to those present and wished them the best as they noted my contact details. As it turned out, they had good backing with sponsors and marketing. They entered Super League in 2006 as the Catalans Dragons. However, by the time they contacted me for the position, Pam and I had decided that the timing didn't suit, and my state of mind was also not ideal.

Over the years since then, they've attracted several high-quality international players. Playing in a competition in another country is a huge struggle, as the NZ Warriors have found in the NRL. Unsurprisingly, the Catalans Dragons have found it tough, although they did beat Warrington in 2018. In doing so, they became the first non-British team to win the Challenge Cup since the competition started in 1896. The club also caused a stir in 2020 by signing Israel Folau who was sacked by Rugby Australia for his statements about same-sex marriage and homosexuality.

My time coaching Tonga was a joy, and it helped me to understand and develop empathy for not only Tongan people but also for Pacific Island people overall. The respect the players afforded me caught me by surprise. I'd done a lot of travelling to other countries before this with representative Rugby League teams, and that certainly didn't cease after the 2000 World Cup.

But each time someone arrives in a country for the first time, there are always surprises, incidents and stories they remember. When that person is a coach, they have the added challenge of keeping the players' focus and commitment on the task at hand. In the next chapter, I'll take you through some of touring's memorable moments, from the Pacific Islands to South Africa and on to Europe.

CHAPTER 6

Touring's Memorable Moments

Daily communication is paramount to create a culture of character and integrity with touring teams.

Touring with sporting teams can create everlasting memories for all involved. It certainly did for me, and judging by the stories from fellow tourists, I'm not the only one. Regardless, whenever we catch up, it reminds me of the games and the humorous events that occurred. But sometimes, having been on so many Rugby League tours to so many countries can cause confusion as to what happened where. Whenever this occurs, it can help to hear the people involved reminisce about their individual tales.

Some of my tours took place before my professional coaching period at the Cowboys, and others occurred afterwards. Between 1993 and 2004, I visited more than one country on some tours and visited some countries more than once. Many trips – including New Zealand, the Cook Islands, Tonga, Samoa, Fiji, Papua New Guinea, South Africa, England, Ireland, Scotland, Wales, France and Great Britain – required me to leave my family behind.

Now, without revealing a diary of daily events, I'd like to divulge some of the anecdotes from those times. I hope you enjoy.

On tour: tough tackling in the Pacific

Fiji

My first overseas tour as a coach was with the Queensland Residents team in 1993, visiting Fiji, Tonga and Samoa. The team was below State of Origin level and comprised players who aspired to play in the NRL premiership. This was the inaugural tour to the Pacific, where Rugby League was being developed and had advanced rapidly over the preceding years.

In this tour, we beat Fiji and Tonga, but lost to Samoa.

The Fijians were extremely fast and elusive. They possessed great attacking skills across the entire squad. However, their tackling ability needed a lot of improvement. They certainly enjoyed the constant collisions, which were more frequent than in their national sport of Rugby Union.

I was, however, surprised at the reaction of the 5,000-strong crowd to frequent head-high tackles by the Fijians. They'd laugh loudly at any incident, so I assume that they didn't understand the risk of damage to a player's spine and brain.

After the match, Prime Minister Sitiveni Rabuka (a former Fijian Rugby Union international himself) and his entourage welcomed us to a post-match function and treated us very well there. This was also my first meeting with Tim Sheens, who was there as a guest coach of the Fiji national team.

Tonga

Our next match, against the Mate Ma'a Tonga at Nuku'alofa, was the most physical of the three we played on tour. However, the Tongan team's physicality and aggression were only evident on the football field. Off the field, they were the most hospitable, respectful people I'd ever come across. I had no idea that, in years to come, I'd actually be coaching this proud nation.

Before the game started, players were called from ground-level to come up the stairs for an acknowledgement from the King of Tonga Taufa'ahau Tupou IV. One of our players was somewhat eager to meet the King. On reaching him, the player tried to stop and his footy boots slipped out from under him, leaving him lying flat on his back at the feet of the King.

The King began to laugh so the entire crowd roared with laughter, and so did we. Unfazed, the next two players in line simply picked our man up and the process continued. But whenever the player ran the ball in our game, the crowd recognised him and cheered again.

The day before the match we were invited to Sunday Mass, at which the King and his family were present. I took the team manager with me, and as we were entering, an administrator stopped me and said, "Please wear a tie, sir. The King is present!"

Needless to say, we complied.

The singing of the congregation and choir at that Mass was delightful. Their harmonising was perfect and seemed natural rather than rehearsed. In fact, I'm not sure whether there was a selected choir at all – people seemed to enter sporadically, some sitting where I assumed the choir was. Thankfully, as I mentioned in the last chapter, this was not the last I'd hear of the magnificent Tongan harmonies.

Samoa

Samoa was much like Fiji and Tonga – a great place to visit with very friendly people who were willing to help in any way. The Samoan players were quite skilful in both attack and defence, but – like the Tongan team when I started coaching – they also lacked aerobic fitness. I could see this clearly in their back-to-back efforts and getting off the ground quickly.

I've said before that it isn't good enough in Rugby League to do something physical well, like tackle, just once. A player must be able to make two, three or even four tackles in succession, back-to-back. Even so, the Samoans won the game – perhaps because our squad was somewhat decimated from one of the physical games the previous week.

Our post-match function for that game was hosted by Prime Minister Tofilau Eti Alesana. And the meal was eventful to say the least.

The seating layout saw me next to the Prime Minister at the centre of the main table. Like most Pacific nations, Samoa relies on natural, fresh food so there was plenty of fish to be consumed at the meal. As a seafood lover, I thought this was wonderful and found myself gulping the fish. Suddenly, a large bone caught in my throat, choking me and turning my face blue.

Luckily, our tour doctor Roy Saunders was at my table and managed to save the situation. Call it revenge or karma, but the players were in hysterics about their coach choking in public. And then the very next mouthful I took of beautiful fish, the same thing happened! Again, a bone lodged in my throat, and again, Roy cleared it.

Since it was the last night on tour, the players – and staff – acted out quite a lot of choking simulations. And I still hear about it from players who were on that tour regularly.

On tour: ripping into the Rhinos

South Africa

The Queensland Residents' tour of South Africa in 1994 was the first time the Queensland Rugby League had sent a team to the Republic. And I was lucky enough to accompany them as coach.

The Queensland Residents team of 1994 – South Africa tour

The calibre of our players on tour was extremely high. They had good skill, tackle technique and leadership through Craig Grauf and Ian Graham. Eleven of this squad also played in the NRL premiership the following year. Some notable names included Travis Norton (Canterbury Bulldogs, NQ Cowboys, Queensland State of Origin), Grant Young (Brisbane Crushers, NZ Warriors, New Zealand), Ian Graham (Canberra Raiders), Craig Grauf (Brisbane Broncos), Steele Retchless (Brisbane

Broncos, English Super League), Shane Christiansen, David Maiden and Brad Tassell (NQ Cowboys) and Craig Spark (Gold Coast).

Johannesburg

Our fullback Steven Craig from Sarina was one of the personalities of the group and it was always obvious he was a country man. People from south of the Queensland border always scoffed at the Queensland drawl and how we said "Ay" at the end of a sentence. As he was checking through customs at Johannesburg airport, Steven handed over his necessary documents. Once he was cleared, he said, "Thanks mate, ay," to the customs officer.

In fact, Steven never spoke without using that "Ay." But I'll never forget the puzzled look on the customs officer's face!

It's often been said that South Africa has great potential for Rugby League, but the sport has a relatively low profile in the country. Instead, Rugby Union is the predominant, more established code. South Africa has competed in two Rugby League World Cups, in 1995 and 2000, and part of our responsibility on tour was to conduct community coaching clinics.

The most memorable clinic was during our visit to Soweto, the township just outside Johannesburg. This area was once a segregated area under apartheid, and it represents the heart of South Africa's 20th-century struggle against injustice.

The enjoyment and excitement on clinic participants' faces was something to behold. I was astonished at the speed at which they picked up drills and the level of ball-handling. They wanted to tackle one another because they'd heard it was a big part of our game. Our players were very good with the participants, mentioning their appreciation of their own lives and hailing the resilience shown by all in Soweto township.

We also played Transvaal at Johannesburg a few days after our arrival. I wondered whether we'd arrived in the land of the giants: the Transvaal team was made up completely of white players, and they were all huge. Luckily for us, while they loved collision, they lacked knowledge of the game, which presented us with a huge win.

Durban

From Johannesburg, we travelled by bus to Durban: a five-hour trip. On the outskirts of Durban, we were positioned behind a car waiting for the lights to turn green. I was seated at the front of the bus and noticed two men come from behind a fence with a pick-handle and baseball bat. They smashed the windscreen of the car, yanked the driver out, hit him unconscious with the bat and stole his car. Shocked, we asked our bus driver if we could do anything to help the man. The driver simply replied, "I saw nothing," then drove off.

The game against Natal in Durban was another strong performance from our group, and I gave some of the younger men more field time. They hadn't played many minutes in our first game: I'd used more experienced players in that one because it was important to start the tour with a win. One of these younger players was Travis Norton, who – at 18 – was the baby of the tour and came from Moranbah. He went on to have a long career and captained the Cowboys.

The younger players were outstanding, and our win in this game was nearly as big as in our first game. It left everyone looking forward to the final game, which was against South Africa's national team, the Rhinos.

At the post-match function for this game, I met the man in charge of South African Rugby League, the entrepreneurial Ockie Oosthuizen. He was an imposing figure with a strong, loud voice to suit his role. His authority and the respect given to him was obvious from the outset. He invited me to his house for lunch one day, and I was amazed at the lavishness of his residence. The property was surrounded by a 2.5-metre high fence with razor wire along the top. He had security gates, guard dogs and sentries for 24 hours each day.

The following day, we travelled to Sun City in the North West Province near Rustenburg, where we stayed. This area is internationally recognised for its resort and themed sub-resorts, including a large, man-made wave pool with beautiful sandy beaches.

Some of the players borrowed my video camera for a while. Then, when I returned home, Pam, Yana and Jarrod were quite surprised to be confronted with girls in nothing but bikinis at the beach in Sun City. Some wore even less. Of course, filming that would be illegal these days.

There was also a beautiful palace, a large casino and an amazing golf course. On the way to Sun City, we drove through Pilanesberg Game Reserve. On either side of the bus we could see giraffes, wildebeest, lions and elephants. Everyone was completely absorbed in the beauty except Steele Retchless who was busy on his Gameboy machine.

When he didn't put it down and look outside after I told him to, I took it from him and threw it out the window – bloody toys!

Back in Johannesburg

Our match against the South African Rhinos at Johannesburg Stadium at Doornfontein in Johannesburg was as tough an affair as expected. The Rhinos were coached by the great Arthur Beetson with Brian Canavan as assistant coach. Brian went on to become CEO of the Sydney Roosters and NRL Head of Football.

Both men had long histories of involvement as top-level players, coaches and administrators, so I expected the Rhinos to be well-drilled and have good game awareness. I impressed upon the Queensland players that this would be their toughest encounter and that we'd need to play until the 80-minute mark.

The Rhinos were certainly motivated for the game. They

displayed great positional play and were well organised. But by midway through the second half, we'd taken control and managed to finish very strongly with a 28–0 win. This tour is still referred to by the players and staff as the most enjoyable three-week period with any group they encountered.

Once again, 'winning solved all problems'.

But I was lucky to go to many other countries as a coach in the coming years too.

On tour: top marks for university students

After coaching Queensland Universities against NSW Universities in 2003 and 2004, I was fortunate to take an Australian representative team on tour to the United Kingdom. This was the first UK tour by an Australian Universities team, which hasn't occurred again since.

France

Touching down in Paris at Charles de Gaulle airport for our first game was exciting for everyone. Unfortunately, after checking through customs and security, one of the players, Michael Giorgas, had his backpack stolen from his baggage trolley. It happened when he turned to talk to some teammates, and the pack contained his passport, money and all identification materials.

It wasn't a good start, delaying us for a couple of hours while the management team helped to arrange a replacement passport and visa. We also had to meet with the embassy, which seemed more an interrogation than an interview. Meanwhile, Michael's parents sent money for the remainder of the tour, and the players often helped him out whenever necessary as well.

Luckily, it wasn't an omen of things to come, and we went through the seven-match tour undefeated.

We played France, England, Ireland, Wales and Scotland, as well as the combined Great Britain Universities team twice. Even though I knew some of the 22 players had played at a reasonably high level before, I didn't know what to expect in terms of the opposition's standard.

The tour took three weeks, and because it was late in the year, several group members found themselves playing in the cold for the first time in their lives.

I thought the game against the French in Paris was probably the toughest of the seven we played, and having a French referee was a hurdle as well. Winning there was a great start, considering the team hadn't played together previously.

England

For this match, we played England at the New River Stadium in North London. This was the home of the London Skolars Rugby League club and was a magnificent field with very good facilities.

Skolars had become a professional club less than two years ago, and the team played like they were unfamiliar with one another. They continually dropped the ball, giving us a lot of possession – a flaw we capitalised on for a 32–6 victory.

Our players had a laugh after the match too, because during the game the English boys continually labelled them 'convicts'. Perhaps they thought it would unsettle us.

Wales

Next, we moved to Cardiff for the Wales game. A shock awaited us there when we couldn't train on the designated ground because the earth and grass were frozen.

I laughed the morning after we arrived when Mick Green from Townsville stepped out of his room and couldn't believe the white grass. He stepped toward it very gingerly and touched it with his foot, wondering what would happen. The coldest temperature we'd ever experienced in a Townsville winter was around 15 degrees Celsius, and there we were with -8 degrees and frost!

The Welsh were very tough physically but lacked direction and skill. This resulted in another good win for us.

Ireland

We stayed – and played – in Limerick for the Irish game. We found ourselves fascinated by the game of Hurling we saw being played on our field just before our match.

In fact, we had a problem getting the players' attention because they were so engrossed. Hurling seemed a risky – if not actively dangerous – game, given that the Hurling stick is shorter than a hockey stick and has a thick blade. Some players termed the game aerial hockey. It seems to me that any game that involves swinging a stick near a person's head would have to be dangerous, and I suspect some of our team's interest came from waiting for someone to inevitably be hit.

Possibly because their focus was still on the Hurling, two of our players were sent off during the first half for what I thought were very trivial incidents. We really struggled as the penalty count mounted against us, causing us to make a mountain of tackles. By the end of that first half, we were down 14–0. However, we recovered in the second half, rediscovering our discipline and completing all sets of six. The Irish struggled in defence, resulting in a 34–14 win for us.

The post-match function was full of singing and Guinness.

By contrast, our trip through to Dublin before we travelled by barge to Scotland was full of interesting history about Northern Ireland. We didn't stay in Dublin or Belfast, but our manager Mike Loftus was English. He explained that Northern Ireland had broken away from Ireland to join the United Kingdom in the early 1900s.

In response, those opposed – Irish nationalists who were generally Catholic – had formed the IRA (Irish Republican Army). So much blood has been shed since this time. Driving through Dublin, we saw evidence of bombed buildings, and streets with razor wire were a common sight in certain areas.

Our bus driver knew exactly where to take us to see what had gone on, telling us about specific events while driving through safe areas. Everyone was very interested.

Scotland

Our barge trip on the Stena line from Belfast to Cairnryan in Scotland took two and a half hours. Gradually, everyone found themselves letting go of the sobering history we'd learnt from our bus driver and enjoying the beautiful weather and scenery.

After boarding the bus at Cairnryan, we arrived in Edinburgh for a couple of days of sightseeing before we played Scotland. Edinburgh Castle was a big hit with the players – especially the re-enactor playing William Wallace out the front. They loved taking photos of him and hearing some of Wallace's notorious lines from the movie Braveheart like, "They can't take our freedom!" I was a little embarrassed when one of the boys showed his naiveté, commenting, "Gees, he must be old. It's a shame to see him this low!"

I was lucky enough later to visit the world-renowned St Andrews golf course, which cost £60 to visit without even playing.

Unfortunately, the time off must not have been good for our team performance, as we really struggled against the Scots. One of the Scottish players developed a compound fracture to his tibia and fibula and an ankle dislocation near the end of the match. This probably affected all players as the final ten minutes were very tepid.

The Scottish team then scored twice against us in the final five minutes of the match, but we held on to win by four points.

These were all tough encounters, made more difficult with the hometown referee each time.

Back to England – playing Great Britain

The tour culminated with our final and most important – two games against Great Britain, both in Halliwell Jones Stadium, home ground of the Warrington Wolves. The Great British team was a representative team with players selected from England, Ireland, Scotland and Wales.

On our journey from Edinburgh down to Warrington, we stayed in York for a couple of days. Training in -4-degree Celsius weather was a real shock to the players.

I met the mayor of Warrington at a meet and greet function, where we swapped notes as I was an elected councillor in Townsville at the time. (My Townsville constituents were aware of my trip and I was entitled to annual leave, so all was approved.) With so many counties and reasonably large cities in England, the government system there is very different to that of Australia, where we have the local, state and federal tiers. Their next level after local government is the House of Commons.

In our final two tests against Great Britain, we initially

sneaked home in our first game, then won convincingly against Great Britain to complete an undefeated tour. Brendan Reeves, our captain, was named 'Players' Player' of the tour. He was the only player with NRL experience (Illawarra Steelers, Manly-Warringah Sea Eagles).

Meanwhile, our strike centre, Jordan Atkins, was signed by the Gold Coast Titans when we returned to Australia. Jordan scored four tries in his NRL debut for the Titans. I was his manager at that time and my phone ran hot with further offers, which he had to weigh up.

After the post-tour function, most players flew to Manchester and from there to Australia, although some stayed on for a holiday. Pam had come over with her English mother and had visited family while doing some touring of her own, so

A happy team after defeating Great Britain in both tests at Warrington

she met me at the function. Together, we joined a Trafalgar tour from London to Rome, then through most of Italy, Switzerland and France, then back to London to return home. We loved every day of this trip. I am very, very grateful to have Pam.

Coaching against other countries should be a proud time for all the fortunate people who do this. Certainly, writing down a few of my stories from along the way has been very pleasing. Being exposed to so many personalities and nationalities in the teams I've been lucky to coach over the years has been so educational and has contributed greatly to my development. Even with the Tongan team Cook Islands tour, the physiotherapist – Yasu (short for Yasuaki) Ichikawa – was Japanese, although his nickname almost sounded Tongan to me.

You don't even need to leave home to experience other cultures. Just coaching Australian teams involves encountering players who are Fijian, Papuan, French, Kiwi, Maori, English, Italian, Greek, Lebanese and, of course, Aboriginal and Torres Strait Islander.

I mentioned earlier how reflecting on tours and stories has been a good reminder of my achievements in Rugby League, and that it's good for the soul and for confidence. But the game has changed in so many ways since those times. I'll discuss where I see it headed, as well as give my thoughts on leadership, in the next chapter.

CHAPTER 7

Coaching, Leadership and Life

> *"Hard choices, easy life. Easy choices, hard life."*
> —Jerzy Gregorek

Hindsight: always 20/20

Now that I've retired from coaching, I can look back and say that I'm proud of my record. It's spanned exactly 23 years from club A-grade games through Queensland representative, Australian representative, NRL and international matches. Taken as a whole, it ended with an overall success rate of 88%.

I only discovered this statistic when I completed my coaching career. I'd never bothered to track my record while coaching – it just wasn't something I considered important at the time.

Thinking about it, I guess my success rate was actually higher than 88% before my appointment as Cowboys' head coach in the NRL premiership in 2001. My coaching methods and philosophies had already been successful with the Cowboys' reserve-grade teams. That's why I'd planned to carry them over to first grade when I became head coach.

Sometimes when people get to the big stage, they forget who showed them how to dance.

The cold, hard reality is that, if we talk ratios of wins and losses (9 wins/26 losses), I was disappointed with my NRL head coach record. I desperately wanted to succeed at the top level and will forever consider it an unfulfilled goal.

As I mentioned back in Chapter 1, coaching an NRL side is one of the toughest gigs in sport – arguably the most cut-throat. So it seems that sacking a coach is the easiest way for a struggling club to look like it's doing something.

Coaches depend on – and deserve – respect from within their clubs, but boardroom politics often don't allow them to do their best. Additionally, coaches are often subject to a lot of negativity from fans and media when their team isn't performing. But the reality is that coaches come into the job with great knowledge and intentions. Sometimes things just don't work out for a variety of reasons – often including being challenged to manage things not only within their control but also outside of it.

As I write this during COVID-19, several other coaches

have been forced out. These include Stephen Kearney (NZ Warriors), Dean Pay (Canterbury Bulldogs), Paul Green (NQ Cowboys), Paul McGregor (St George Dragons) and Anthony Seibold (Brisbane Broncos)

I know Anthony Seibold well, and found it distressing to see him – and his family – being dragged through the social media sewer. He's a decent, intelligent human being who didn't deserve what the faceless cowards on keyboards threw at him. Having the Broncos' largest private investor compare Anthony to a cancer that needs to be cut out before the Broncos die was an absolute disgrace.

We don't need people like that in our game – or in sport in general.

The emergence of Tonga

This was a real contrast to the respect that the Tongan players and administrators showed me when I was appointed national coach of Tonga in 1998.

At first, I thought that this respect was born from my coaching position at the Cowboys. I was someone who'd been coaching at the highest level, now steering the Tongan players in their own country. But even when they got to know me as an average person, the respect continued. I could have asked or shown them anything, and they would have tried to please. They never stopped giving their best.

I honestly didn't treat Australian players very differently

from Tongan players. With both types of players, I was confident in what I instructed. The difference was that the Tongan players had been through various development systems that resulted in them always wanting and expecting to learn new things. Many of the Australian players thought they already knew everything, while no Tongan I ever coached had this attitude. Normally, these were occasions where the player needed to 'pull their head in'. If they wanted to argue, I'd simply say, "If I agreed with you, we'd both be wrong."

Today, looking back on those years revives memories of some of my fondest and most satisfying times in Rugby League. In fact, I'd like to think I played a small part in developing what Tonga has become today: an international Rugby League powerhouse.

Following the country's shock 16–12 win over world champions Australia in 2019, I was thrilled to receive texts from several members of the Tongan team I coached in 1998–2000.

Among the well-known players who texted – all of whom had played extensively in the NRL and had also represented Tonga – were:

- **Tevita Koloi,** team manager back then: *"What we are watching now is the benefits of your work with our country in the late 1990s and World Cup. Bless you, Murray."*

- **Brent Kite:** *"You started this, mate."*

👟 **Phil Howlett:** *"Congrats to Tonga and to you, Murray."*

👟 **Andrew Lomu:** *"Thanks for your work, Murray."*

Being recognised for my contribution some 20 years after I coached Tonga was indeed a privilege.

Leaders in action

Leading both by voice and by actions is the key attribute of a leader. I think good leaders not only get to know each player's personality but also watch them closely at training to gauge their strengths and their ethics.

Coaches also have the advantage of mixing with teammates socially. This enables them to understand how to address each player in the 'heat of battle'. The skipper must always deliver a performance at the level of at least 7–9 out of 10 in every game. Something I always noticed at functions with a team was that players would inevitably file in behind the captain, practically pushing them to the front. The captain is the person who addresses the public or the media (and if they don't have the skills initially, they could always have tutoring).

All of these points are normally noticeable traits of a leader.

To determine a prospective leader, I watched the playing group closely during training sessions and meetings. A couple of people would normally stand out as potential candidates. Their peers listened to them. They showed that they were on the same wavelength as me regarding how I wanted the game played. And they maintained their teammates' respect.

This could occur with players I hadn't previously regarded as leadership material.

For example, I'd put the Melbourne Storm's Cameron Smith in this category. His teammates do as he says because they know he has the big picture in his mind, and he always puts in 100% effort. He also knows the role of all positions and each player's strengths.

Cameron is a rarity in this regard. He's also the smartest player I've ever seen.

Another classic example is Mark Graham, the great Kiwi backrower. Mark didn't play any junior representative Rugby League in New Zealand, but went on to represent his country in 29 tests, 18 of them as captain. He was named Player of the Century (1907–2006) for his country.

Mark led by his actions on the field through strong running and great defence, and he developed into an outstanding captain. He was an outstanding coach as well, and was assistant coach at the Cowboys in the early years.

The Benne-factor

Another leader I still stand in awe of is Wayne Bennett. My association with Wayne began in 1991 – my fourth year of coaching. He asked me to join his support staff at the Brisbane Broncos and coach Brothers in the Brisbane Rugby League competition. Taking up this role required Pam, the children and I to move from Mackay to Brisbane.

The Broncos finished seventh that year but went on to win the first-grade premiership in 1992 and 1993 with Bennett at the helm. Brothers, basically a feeder club to the Broncos, had come close to folding since their premiership win in 1987. However, they'd had an improved year in 1991 with quite a few players gaining their debut and finishing one win out of the final four.

From our first meeting, Wayne and I got on well. We seemed to have similar views on football and life. Here was someone who already stood tall in Rugby League throughout Queensland and Australia. And I now consider him the doyen of coaches: nobody has won as many premierships and been to so many grand finals.

Winning seven NRL premierships and several State of Origin series is the epitome of success and longevity for a coach. I'm amazed that a person can coach so long at the top and still be able to relate to several generations of players. People and players change as the years roll on, but Wayne has continually adapted to and empathised with whomever he's been involved with.

People say that players aren't as tough now as they were in the 1960s to 1980s. However, those in the know – as both Wayne and I are – will beg to differ. And I believe Wayne Bennett is the most qualified person to have an informed opinion on this.

More coaching moves

I made the tough decision to move on from the Broncos and Brothers after only one year. My priority was spending time with my young family. My coaching roles in Brisbane required spending two nights at Broncos training plus the Sunday game, and three nights at Brothers training plus the Saturday game. This meant I left home each day at 7 am and didn't get back till 9 pm, truly leaving little family time. So I was extremely grateful to Norths Rugby League Club – and its secretary Peter Hunt – for appointing me as coach of the Rockhampton club in 1992.

The 1992, 1993 and 1994 seasons at Norths were some of the most enjoyable of my coaching career. I'd actually played for the club for ten years from 1974 as a five-eighth and centre. Returning as coach in 1992 was a privilege, although I had a tough task ahead of me. Norths hadn't won a game in 1991, and in three games they'd been beaten by over 100 points.

However, the rest – as they say – is history. We went on to win the Rockhampton premiership in all three years, losing only six games in that time. We also won the Central Queensland Extended League premiership in all three years.

I believe a key reason for this success was making sure I was close to the players. I mentioned earlier that I enjoyed showing players new things. Norths needed a total rebuild, making those 'new things' essential. To shake up the status quo, I moved players into unfamiliar positions so I could show them how I believed they should play in their new role.

I also used skill-drills at training as a means of fast-tracking their development. Their enjoyment and acceptance of all the new techniques and game plans proved to be the recipe for on-field success. However, I also can't overstate the sense of togetherness that Pam and I created when we had players over at our home for various games – often just chatting together. They felt very comfortable. I know Pam enjoyed it as well, and Yana and Jarrod still talk about it. These could well have been my most satisfying years of coaching.

Graham White, whom I made captain of Norths, was probably one of the smartest players I coached at any level. He also represented Central Queensland Capras, Queensland Country and Queensland Residents, as well as being the Cowboys reserve-grade Player of the Year in 1996.

In 1995, I decided to switch camps in Rockhampton from Norths to Brothers. I wanted a new challenge, and we (Brothers) had won the premiership, beating Norths in the grand final and winning 24 of our 26 games that year. This was a very difficult move, given that I'd played at Norths a long time and coached them to premierships.

Being Brothers arch-rivals, Norths were – and probably still are – very disappointed. My 'desertion' made them hate Brothers even more, and I knew they'd look on me as a traitor. This was evidenced in the first game of the season where we clashed. My very good mate Darryl Horstman, who'd been a Norths man all his life, had the Norths boys ready, and their catch-cry during the game was, "Muz!"

Coaching Queensland Country in 1990

In the end, in a very tough game, Norths beat Brothers by 32–12. In a strange way, I wasn't disappointed because I didn't think Norths would be able to lift the way they did. Plus, they achieved their goal of 'rubbing it in' to me. They played me.

That said, it was the only time they beat us, and we beat them on Grand Final day.

Before that, in the early- to mid-90s, I'd done other coaching stints that I was proud of. I guided Queensland Country in 1990 to wins over Papua New Guinea, NSW Country and France. Then, in 1993, we played one game, beating our Brisbane city counterparts.

The Queensland Residents Rugby League team are at the level below the State of Origin team. There was, and still is, a traditional interstate game each year. It was played as a curtain-raiser to the State of Origin game. At the end of each season, there was also a tour for the Residents to commit to if they were selected.

I coached the Queensland Residents team for three years from 1993 to 1995, and I documented two tours I did with them in the previous chapter. By the time the 1995 team toured at the end of the season, I was already at the Cowboys. I also coached the unbeaten Central Queensland Capras team in 1993–1995, as well as the Rockhampton Rustlers in the state league competition in 1995.

In 1995 alone, I coached in over 40 games, of which we lost only three. Sometimes, I'd even coach two or three games on a weekend – one for Rockhampton, another for Central Queensland and a third for Rockhampton Rustlers. The Rustlers included players from Rockhampton only and not from other leagues in Central Queensland. (The Queensland Residents v NSW was always a mid-week game.)

Winning the Queensland State League with the Rockhampton Rustlers was a great achievement, as we had to beat Brisbane Rugby League teams as well as North Queensland and Gold Coast. The Brisbane teams were semi-professional and appeared to be a cut above those in the league network. Any loss along the way meant elimination.

1995 was the final year of the State League competition before it was renamed the Queensland Cup. I'll never forget the effort and commitment of the players and staff who represented Rockhampton. It was a great achievement by everyone involved, and one I still hold in very high regard today due to the 'local flavour' of players and support staff.

However, my family must have wondered if I'd ever be at home. I know they lost track of who I was coaching and when. At the time I didn't see it because I was totally obsessed with coaching. I loved it and never tired of it. Nowadays, I can't believe I was so selfish: it would have been OK to decline one or more of the offers to coach. I didn't like letting down the people who asked me to coach, though, so I ended up letting my family down instead. Thank God Pam stuck by me.

Eventually, in late 1995, I moved my family back to Townsville to begin my professional coaching career with the Cowboys, which I detailed in Chapter 1. Meanwhile, I was also busy coaching the other teams I've talked about in previous chapters.

I never anticipated getting a second opportunity at NRL level after foregoing the Broncos/Brothers four years earlier. I've always been grateful to Tim Sheens for appointing me and giving me the chance to work with him. If he hadn't asked me to come to the Cowboys with him, I don't believe there would have been anything for me in the future. And asking me to go there a year before his arrival to monitor development was so trusting of him.

At that point, I was happy with what I'd achieved already and just didn't expect the offer.

Then, in 1997, my Australia Under-17 team played the New

A great achievement by the Rockhampton Rustlers – Queensland State League champions in 1995

Zealand Under-18 team – which surprised me, given that the Kiwis were all a year older. As it was, I believed New Zealand to be the land of the giants. Admittedly, though, the size equation balanced out somewhat with six of our forwards being over 100 kg. And I couldn't believe the amount of food they ate during the five-day stay at the hotel!

This game was a curtain-raiser to the Queensland v NSW game, and our team won by 16 points. Several players in our team had played higher levels in senior football. Players who

*With the Australian Under 17-team after the
game against New Zealand in 1997*

went on to achieve State of Origin honours a few years down the track included Dane Carlaw, Carl Webb, Josh Hannay, Chris Walker, Willie Mason and Scott Prince. All played test football for Australia except Chris and Josh, who was captain of the Australian team and went on to coach at Queensland Cup level. He then took over the interim head coaching role at the Cowboys at the end of the 2020 season.

I was also lucky enough to cross paths again with Wayne Bennett. As Queensland State of Origin coach, he appointed me as coach of the Emerging State of Origin squad for 2000 and 2001. Nine players from that squad went on to play for the State of Origin team in 2001, which beat NSW convincingly by 34–16 in Game #1 and 40–14 in Game #3. This was another masterstroke by Wayne to debut so many young players on such a stage. It was fantastic.

Additionally, I was very proud and pleased to watch John Doyle and John Buttigieg both debut in the first Origin game, and to see both of them score tries. I'd coached them since 1996. Paul Bowman – whom I talked about in Chapter 1 – was also a fixture in the team. What a player!

After losing the head coaching position at the Cowboys early in 2002, I had no more involvement until I was invited to coach the Queensland Universities representative team against NSW in 2003. We defeated them by the biggest margin since inception. This was my only coaching that year as I realised that my coaching had started to take precedence over everything else in my life.

Despite my coaching success, one thing remained constant: my wife and children were far more important to me than my career as a coach.

The next year in 2004, however, I picked up the reins again in Townsville, guiding Brothers to the A-grade premiership in the Townsville & District Rugby League competition. This was a great homecoming for me since my 1988 coaching debut had been with Brothers.

Everyone – from the club to the town and all of Queensland Rugby League – seemed to expect me to take them to a premiership win because of my history. However, I didn't feel any pressure to succeed, and I instilled this relaxed approach into the group. Despite not having won the competition in more than ten years, the team ended up winning the premiership.

I also coached the Queensland Universities team that year, and they too won this time.

Later in 2004, I came close to heading overseas to coach English Super League team Castleford for their 2005 season. The club contacted me to gauge my interest, and I thought it might have been worth a shot. I flew to England for ten days at Castleford to set up a playing roster and support staff and spend some time with the board. They offered a three-year contract, but I decided against it in the end – for family, health and business reasons.

After that, I didn't coach again until 2007, when I guided the Townsville Brothers Under-19 team. This was an enjoyable assignment, as I could show young men the way with footy and life. We had a successful season winning the premiership while losing only one game along the way.

My business career then took me to Mackay in 2008, which I documented in Chapter 3, to manage the construction company (amongst the other roles I talked about). And during that time, I constantly had two jobs: one in business and one in coaching.

Then in 2010, after a year off coaching, I assisted Leigh McWilliams at Townsville Brothers with the A grade. I'd coached Leigh at the Cowboys and thought he was a good man. I also coached the Under-18 team that year – a rewarding experience because the young men were so eager to listen. We won both premierships that year.

I wanted to wrap up my coaching life in 2011 once and for all, so again, I took the A-grade reins at Townsville Brothers. We'd retained the majority of the previous year's premiership team, including Michael Green, Roy Baira, Scott Dowd and Adam Peluchetti from the 2004 premiership-winning team I'd coached. This made me feel quite nostalgic, but I was also eager to bring a good number of juniors through to the top grade.

And, indeed, we dominated the competition again, winning the premiership convincingly.

In addition to all of this, I coached the Queensland University representative team against NSW that year for a 10–all draw.

A bloody good leader

The news that Ian Roberts was going to play for the Cowboys in 1997 was a very exciting revelation for me, the club and the entire North Queensland region. Even though I hadn't met Ian, I'd loved the toughness I'd seen him display every time I watched him for Souths, Wigan and Manly. This carried over into his representative career with NSW and playing 14 test matches for Australia.

I was nervous about meeting him initially due to my high regard for him. So it was a pleasant surprise to discover he displayed a humble manner and obvious integrity.

Two years prior, Ian had come out as a gay man – the first League player ever to publicly reveal his sexuality. This also epitomised his toughness, given that he was such a huge figure in Rugby League. Unfortunately, not everyone was as excited as I was about his arrival. One prominent Northern politician said publicly that he'd never go to a game or support the Cowboys while 'that man' was there. His loss!

Concentration on the sideline in 2000

When Tim Sheens named Ian as Club Captain, I – and thousands of his supporters – were over the moon. It was an excellent call. Ian was great in the community and his partner got on well with everyone so it was a good decision.

Initially, the Cowboys' acceptance of Ian was tense – at least until he broke the ice one day in a team meeting. Some of the less tolerant players were having a bit of a dig at him for being gay, and one said, "Well, you won't get me, Robbo!" Not missing a beat, Ian replied, "Don't flatter yourself! You're not my type." That broke the tension and relaxed the whole room – it was such a pivotal moment.

Unfortunately, that wasn't the end of the bigotry Ian experienced. I remember another occasion where I was showing a newly signed player to his locker. I told him he could have the locker next to Ian or a different one next to Steve Walters. He immediately said, "Uh, uh, I'll take this one," and pointed to the locker furthest from Ian's.

It's sad how people used to assume so much in those days. Luckily, there's less stigma now.

Despite the rocky start, Ian's popularity in the club grew quickly because he combined leadership, toughness and ability to impart knowledge gained through experience to younger players. One of the toughest things I saw him do, both mentally and physically, was during the interstate tri-series of 1997. On the Wednesday night, he played front-row for NSW against

Queensland. Then on the Saturday, he backed up to captain the Cowboys against the Broncos at QE2 in Brisbane.

On the Wednesday, he'd played most of the NSW game. Then, during the Broncos game, we'd been behind all game but were starting to come back at the tail-end and led by four points inside the last minute. Steve Renouf, one of the quickest ever players and still the Broncos' leading try scorer, broke away down the sideline with 75 metres to run. If he'd scored near the posts, we'd have been beaten: the try would have levelled the teams, and converting it would have given them the win.

Ian chased their quickest player – never stopping – and his determination kept Steve out wide the full distance, forcing him to score in the corner. The Broncos missed the kick, and we ended up drawing with them. It was incredible – I don't know anyone else who could have made such an effort. He was respected enormously.

Ian played one more year at the Cowboys, then – sadly – announced his retirement from the game after the 1998 season.

More than just being an incredible player, Ian Roberts is a man of unwavering integrity and honesty. I believe that any person who spends time with him will come away with a much more balanced attitude to life. I've been present at some of his talks: he holds the crowds very well as they await his every word. He's also a professional actor.

Over the past nine years, I've been happy when my role as welfare manager with the NRL in Queensland has meant we've occasionally crossed paths. Ian now runs a group of theatre sports actors, who act out certain predicaments that players might have or encounter in society. The players absolutely love this: they get the messages so much better through this medium because the situation is more realistic.

All in all, he's a bloody good bloke.

With Ian Roberts at a Rugby League Wellbeing and Education conference in 2019

Where League is headed

The Rugby League ethos has been under scrutiny for quite some time and I really don't know what the game will become in the next two to three decades. It used to appeal to all socio-economic levels because it was basically 'the survival of the fittest'. Whichever team held onto the ball longest would win. It also epitomised the common Australian theme of hard work and commitment, and was something people could associate with and therefore aspire to play.

At that time, the best team would always be the one that had the edge in either skill, strength, speed, fitness or smarts. Today, all these traits are now common to every team. These days, sports psychology has become a major, with sports science telling coaches and support staff anything and everything they can use as an advantage.

Having a 'great player' in your squad is another enormous advantage. Coaches are forever trying to be inventive and get the edge. Where we once spoke of a 'good tackle on the ball-carrier' when discussing defence, such terms as 'the wrestle', 'the dismount', 'the dance' and 'the cuddle' have all now emerged. (Those last two really worry me.)

To explain, 'the wrestle' came into the game as a result of players becoming very adept at offloading the ball whilst being tackled. This created a lot of urgency and pressure for the defending team as often, after an offload, the ball is shifted to spaces where defenders are struggling to realign. To prevent this from occurring, a need arose to have two, sometimes three, tacklers involved. The additional two would lock up the ball to keep it from being offloaded.

I recall Mark Graham calling this 'the dance' when we coached together at the Cowboys. It was so-called because players appeared to be standing and 'cuddling' the person with the ball before forcing them to the ground, thus effecting the tackle. The two or three tacklers would then have to get to their feet quickly to be at the marker position, hence the 'dismount' off the tackled player.

I strongly suspect these terms came from old-timers secretly having a dig at the current players. The truth is that all players are more skilful now than when we played.

Meanwhile, the advent of psychologists and sports scientists can only advance the game with regard to player safety, mental health and fitness. Coaches continually try to find the 'edge' over their rivals. They implement their ideas by adding specific professionals to their staff. The costs of these new trends have affected the costs of managing clubs enormously over time. And there's always robust discussion as to whether it's better to have a good athlete or a tough person who can morph into a good player.

On top of all that, rule changes also seem to be part of the framework now. People in the know are continually trying to devise changes that will speed up the game and consequently make it more attractive for viewers. I understand that some changes are made to increase the game's appeal to the viewers, and perhaps to grow the supporter base to compete with other sports, which equates to marketing.

However, I believe that we must solidify the rules to make the game simple for the players, referees and supporters, after which the sport will dominate the world over. Plus, players and spectators both love collision in sport. As I've mentioned before, Rugby League has the most brutal contact as well as unrivalled skill and ever-increasing speed. What a fantastic recipe!

Whilst I never expected to coach for long at all, I enjoyed my career from 1988 to 2011, with the odd year off in between. And this would not have been possible if Pam hadn't been so supportive. For someone who doesn't like Rugby League, she's been very patient with me as I've continued my hobby. Although one thing she always enjoyed were the stories I brought home, whether they were from local, representative or national coaching.

When I try to decipher how I managed to have so much success, I recognise that my method of being personable carried so much weight. Sure, my knowledge of the game was very good, but I could also simplify the game and address any issues that arose. Additionally, I realise now that the work I did back then laid the foundation for what I'd do as Wellbeing and Education Manager with the NRL later on.

Perhaps the biggest thing I've realised in my 20+ years of coaching is that what a person learns after they think they know it all is the most important lesson.

In the next chapter, I'll explain more about how this unfolds.

CHAPTER 8

Suicides, Sagas and Social Media

The choices you make, in all aspects of your life, will either make or break you.

The mental health knife-edge

When I started coaching back in 1988, and certainly before then when I was playing, nobody talked about mental health. There was a real public stigma attached to mental struggles. People with depression were labelled with hurtful names such as 'nutter' or 'psycho', so any Rugby League players who were in a dark place kept it to themselves.

Part of this was because they played a collision sport and had a tough persona to uphold. If someone turned up at training apparently bothered by something, players around that person would commonly say things like, "Toughen up, sunshine. We gotta train now, we gotta train well and we gotta play on Sunday."

But in 2015, attitudes like this led to five player suicides and a death on the field, all in the space of only four months. This created a crisis point for me in my role as NRL Wellbeing and Education Manager for Queensland. And by the end of the year, I was close to breaking point myself.

I'd taken on the job in 2012, priding myself on my mental toughness, especially after some of the challenges I'd faced in my 20-year coaching career. However, those suicides – two of them on successive nights – and the on-field death really had me on the knife-edge mentally.

I was totally spent and needed help.

A psychologist told me I had 'compassion fatigue', but I knew that the grieving families, friends and staff at the clubs appreciated the support that I and the NRL provided. And yet, somehow, I couldn't let go of what happened. I absorbed everything: everyone else's problems and feelings. I wasn't a trained psychologist, so I just had to handle everything as best I could as far as my own life experiences were concerned.

But to this day, I still feel deep sorrow for the families involved. It's not surprising that I needed professional help to get over the devastation. Mental health is certainly not an area where anyone should compare the impact or seriousness of incidents – and losing a player will always be extremely tough.

One of the incidents involved a young man on contract to an NRL club who was highly regarded as a future leader, and who had sustained a training injury. There's never a good time to get injured, but this was particularly inopportune as he was about to make his debut in the top grade. He struggled to handle the very slow recuperation, and psychologically he wasn't in a good place, so he returned to his family in his hometown for support.

Unfortunately, this didn't lift his state of mind. So, believing there was no solution, he took his life.

I immediately flew to his hometown and spent a few days with his family, whom I hadn't known before the event. I discovered that sometimes, there's no need to say anything initially. The important thing is simply to be there for the grieving person. Often, a simple touch – perhaps a gentle hug – is the best method to establish trust. Ultimately, this may advance to a few words before growing into a long discussion.

Understandably, this young man's mother and sisters were, and still are, all emotionally devastated. The trust I built with them that day has transformed into a strong friendship, which remains solid to this day.

His mother has since been called upon from time to time to address young people who expect to have bright futures in their field. Talking to others in this way can be healing for some people, although only the person impacted can decide whether it's right for them. From the outside, she seems to be managing now – but, of course, only she knows the reality of her situation.

We all know that grief never truly leaves.

As a repercussion of this sad situation, a couple of the

player's mates who were part of a very tight-knit group tried to replicate his attempts. This effect is known as 'suicide contagion'. Perhaps they subconsciously believed that, since the player couldn't find any reason to live, they didn't want to continue without him.

Thankfully, none of these later attempts was successful. And the good news is that wellbeing staff working in the region and at the club offered these mates assistance to address their state of mind. Coaches and support staff are now well-schooled in this area as well.

Doing the job that needs to be done

Another incident involved the suicide of a senior player at one of the clubs. I received a distraught call from the club CEO on a Saturday afternoon to report the suicide and ask me what he should do. I told him to assemble all registered players and their families, and that I'd be there with them at 9am the next day.

Entering the room and seeing upwards of 90 people not just sad but actually sobbing was something I'd never encountered before in my career. My first reaction would normally be to cry as well, but this situation demanded that at least one person and voice stay strong.

I quickly discovered that nobody had realised the young man had been having any problems. It later came to light that he'd been gambling, which can affect everyone in a person's life – but as far as people knew at the time, everything had been fine. He'd even just bought a block of land with his fiancée.

During my talk to the group, I recommended being very conscious of their behaviours and attitudes over the coming days and weeks. In particular, I cautioned them to:

- reduce or eliminate alcohol
- be aware of their partner and family, and make a point of talking to them and spending more time with them
- check on their teammates daily
- meet up with their mates outside of the club
- ensure that they slept well
- stay very aware when they were driving as they could expect their minds to wander (for this, I recommended concentrating as if they were driving on L-plates).

I'd also arranged for a psychologist to address the group after me, and hearing her reiterate my recommendations gave me some comfort.

After my talk, I spent time individually with players and staff. The atmosphere in the room was difficult to describe. Most people looked blankly around at others for direction on how to carry themselves. I can only assume that they were in shock – much like soldiers in combat who'd lost their mates.

I was particularly saddened that the young player's brother and sister-in-law were present. I can't imagine how difficult this must have been for them. No one ever knows how another person will grieve. In fact, nobody knows how they themselves will grieve or how long their grief will take.

My day ended at around 6pm that day. I remember feeling very drained, although I can't recall driving from the club in Brisbane to our home on the Sunshine Coast. Pam immediately detected my distress, and wanting to help, she started talking to me about other things. I felt awful saying it, but at the time, I just wanted her to be there without talking.

I'm so lucky that she's always there.

Then, only two weeks later, I stood in another room with a similar number of people who all wore the same blank look. I don't want to describe the entire situation again, but I can say that it was no easier the second time around.

Sometimes, I wonder what impact it had on me to suppress my feelings and natural reactions so I could be strong for the people I needed to support through my job.

Educating players and breaking down stigma

Professional and semi-professional players are informally expected to be role models to young players – and to young people in society generally. I certainly don't want to condone bad behaviour or make excuses for it, but players never sign a second contract saying that they now agree to be a role model. Players are under pressure to perform from parents, partners, managers and even themselves. I believe that all any player should ever be concerned about is training to the best of their ability and playing to their best.

Players' choices impact more than just themselves – there are family, extended family, workmates, teammates and – depending on their position – possibly hundreds of other people.

To help with this pressure, my Wellbeing team has offered many lectures and presentations on drugs, alcohol, social media, domestic violence, gambling, respect and resilience over the years. And these have been well received by one and all, with

Presenting to 640 players in 2016

both staff and players appreciating the messages. However, I believe there should always be more follow-up in one-on-one situations, rather than simply running a presentation and ticking a box.

Our mantra was always to address and break down the stigma of mental health and suicide. Thankfully, this has started to happen in Rugby League with all clubs now willing to welcome discussion and prevention methods.

I mentioned in the previous chapter that sometimes, rather than doing a set presentation, we introduced the kind of theatre sports that Ian Roberts does to communicate the messages. Some of the skits that the professional theatre sports actors act out include:

- A player at a nightclub being confronted by a scantily dressed woman who wants to take photographs in a compromising position. These photographs might then go up on various social media platforms, leading to all types of accusations.
- A player of note unknowingly having a bag of drugs pushed into their pocket, and the perpetrator then reporting that the player is distributing drugs.
- A player being confronted and challenged by a man who punches him to incite a fight.
- A player who is out to dinner with their partner being continually harassed by supporters one after another.

- ⚽ Another player who is out to dinner being befriended by the restaurateur to the extent of being showered with gifts or free meals in exchange for photographs.
- ⚽ A player who'd lost form on the field being belittled by their partner, and feeling under pressure both at home and in their job. This can lead to anxiety and depression, and can affect their form to the extent of losing their contract.
- ⚽ A player spending time in gambling outlets where they gradually become blasé with the size of their bets and grow obsessed with recovering lost funds until they are hooked.
- ⚽ An injured player who can't train spending all their time at the physio, surgeon or doctor without seeing their mates. This can lead to them becoming reclusive, and developing issues of isolation, depression and anxiety.

Each of these skits would last just 15–30 minutes. Afterwards, the facilitator would describe what had just happened and encourage players to talk about what the 'player' could have done differently to change the situation. Every skit resulted in these conversations – although it wasn't always a senior player who instigated the discussion. After all, these issues are mostly societal.

The most confronting skits I've seen involve a woman who's been sexually assaulted (gang raped) being interviewed by police. The actress describes the incident from start to finish. She makes her statement to the police, but talks more about her feelings and what she experienced during and since the attack. She has tears rolling down her face – often sobbing uncontrollably for the 15-minute duration of her monologue. I've seen four different ladies acting this role, and they were all brilliant.

Every single time, as the actress addressed the group of 40 to 60 players and staff, I could see their mouths drop open in disbelief and sympathy.

> *The question I asked the players afterwards is certainly not, "What would you do if you were a perpetrator?" but instead, "What would you do if the victim was your sister, your partner, your mother or another relative?"*

In our presentations, we recommended stating, "This is not your fault. You're safe now," and "I'm here for you." Then ask, "What can I do to help?" After we shared these statements, my co-facilitator and good mate David Solomona would tell the group that he has a wife and three daughters. He explains how he would feel and react to re-enforce the messages, which always holds the group's attention even more.

> *As a result, the young players very much absorb and adopt the message of 'respect for women'.*

Discipline and decency

In recent years, instances of players behaving badly have increased dramatically, and Rugby League's public image has taken a battering. Scandals have ranged from sex to assaults, drunkenness, violence against women, gambling, drug-taking and drink-driving. Great front-page headlines for the media!

We need to take the strongest possible action to rid the code of offenders who display reckless stupidity. The same is true for anyone who ignores the ethical standards that need to be upheld for Rugby League to thrive as a code that the community strongly supports. Players now receive ample education and guidance on how to act responsibly, so they have no excuses.

While I feel great empathy for anyone with mental health problems, this empathy doesn't extend to ill-disciplined players who damage Rugby League's image through their bad behaviour.

I think the advent of Super League in 1996 caused a lot of behavioural problems in Rugby League. News Ltd started

Super League as a breakaway competition that lasted only one season. Suddenly, players started being paid ten times more than they'd been earning before, so they had no need for any other employment. When all they had to do was play Rugby League, they had a lot of spare time on their hands.

To be fair, it must be noted that most players *do* stay out of trouble. In fact, less than 1% of players in the NRL and Intrust Super Cup get into strife. The problem is that, in the public eye, players are labelled as role models. But while they're schooled on social interaction they don't get any mentorship training.

And when it comes to behavioural issues, I must also point to social media, which I strongly believe has become the root of all evil. It creates the four D's: Distraction, Displacement, Division and Depression. The truth is that we're in an age where many people's lives are tied to social media platforms. Sites like Facebook and Twitter – and their legions of opinionated 'experts' – have infiltrated every part of our existence – even the areas that used to be private and sacred.

If you compare yourself to others, especially on social media, you will always be unfulfilled.

Social media has given people the opportunity to stand out from the crowd and achieve viral status online. Through it, users can freely insult, berate, provoke and abuse each other.

Sexting, in particular, has destroyed many relationships. One sexting case I know of led to a young man's suicide.

On top of this, the 2020 NRL season's commencement was delayed due to the COVID-19 pandemic. This meant that players had more time on their hands and coaches needed to reschedule preparations. During this time, four prominent players – Latrell Mitchell, Josh Addo-Carr, Nathan Cleary and Tyronne Roberts-Davis – posted videos to social media that showed they weren't social-distancing and following government protocol. All four players were fined and handed suspended bans.

Well-known journalist Paul Kent summed up the situation well in late April 2020 on *Fox League Live*, saying:

> It's not because they don't know, or they're naïve. It's arrogance. They think they're above the law. They get mollycoddled their whole lives, so when the rest of society has to shut down, these guys don't think it applies to them... They should be crucified.

I couldn't agree more with his comments.

Wellbeing on and off the field

Back when I started as Wellbeing and Education Manager for Queensland NRL in 2012, I was the only person doing the job. It shows the level of importance now placed on player welfare and behaviour that by the end of 2019, I had 17 people working with me in Queensland. Our target area was the Intrust Super

Cup – the second-tier competition – which involved 14 clubs and around 680 players.

Our work has always been about prevention rather than reaction, but we all know that the incident count will probably never be zero.

For each player we do a wellbeing plan that incorporates a 'flourishing scale', then we revisit that plan three times a year. The scale provides a psychological wellbeing score based on the player's self-perceived success in important areas such as relationships, self-esteem, purpose and optimism.

Young people's resilience is one of the larger issues in this day and age. To enhance that resilience, our wellbeing program focuses on empathy, gratitude and mindfulness. Respect for teammates, partners and superiors is another attribute we aim to instil in players through education. It's all about them becoming better people during and after their playing career.

A problem for many players is that they live an insular existence as professional footballers, then have trouble adjusting to life during retirement. A critical part of our work is career guidance so that players know where they're headed once their playing days are over.

A lot of players now realise that Rugby League should be their Plan B and not Plan A.

We invite all contracted players to be part of our 'Career Wise' program, which tailors one-on-one career support to their individual stage of career planning. The program comprises a minimum of four career meetings each year and includes several initiatives to enhance the player's life after football.

In short, the work the NRL puts into helping current and retiring players is massively understated.

Developing mental health awareness is an ongoing process, as is building resilience. I pay homage to both David Solomona and Trish Walding for helping me to improve these most important facets of wellbeing for Rugby League players and staff throughout Queensland. Their passion and belief in how we taught this was great.

The two competitions below NRL in Queensland – Intrust Super Cup and Hastings Deering Colts – are full of talented footballers, many of whom make their NRL debuts each year. There are also plenty of players who've achieved off the field in these competitions. In fact, there were at least 60 players studying for post-Rugby careers in 2019.

There's an edict in Rugby League at this level that players must be either studying or working in order to play each game. If an individual drops out of their course or work in any given week, they cannot be selected to play.

Some of the courses and qualifications achieved with this

policy are well worth noting. Vocationally, players who've already qualified include:

- lawyers (3)
- physiotherapists (2)
- structural engineers (2)
- aircraft technician (1)
- teachers (12)
- teacher aides (21)
- accountants (5)
- bank tellers (3)
- tradesmen (22)
- apprentices (21).

As these players are all at a semi-professional level and are committed to their post-Rugby League futures, I have enormous respect for them.

As manager of the Queensland State of Origin Under-20 team in 2016 and as NRL Wellbeing and Education Manager, I attempted to have these educational achievements highlighted in the media. I sent the story to six separate newspapers, but not one published it – unbelievable! If there'd been a controversy, the story would have been both front- and back-page news.

At times, some members of the media seem to exhibit ethics

that make them very difficult to trust. They have enormous power in what they print. For example, many people read a tabloid article, then take it as gospel. That same person can hear the same story in a conversation and not believe it because it is 'someone else's opinion'. The public always chooses what they believe is factual.

But controversy gets people's attention. Controversy sells newspapers. The good news is that I've heard people say they only believe half of what they read in the newspaper, so maybe change is afoot.

Helping the Australian Rugby Union team

In my role as a mental health advocate, one of the most interesting and worthwhile missions I've embarked on was with the Australian Stockman Rugby Union team. I was with the team on its 2017 tour to New Zealand and Argentina.

I joined the tour as both a skills development coach and a voice to educate the players on suicide, depression and domestic violence. The team was selected from country players from Australia's remote, rural and regional areas, and had Wallaby legend Chris Roche as its head coach.

With the support of Wallaby legends and Super Rugby players, the Australian Stockman Rugby program provides development opportunities for grassroots talent. At the same time, it raises awareness about men's health. This is a great initiative, especially when legendary ambassadors like John Eales, Mark Ella and Michael O'Connor get involved.

John and Mark are worldwide greats of Rugby Union. John, a Marist College Ashgrove old-boy, captained the Wallabies for many years and led them to their 1999 World Cup victory. Mark is not only revered as a great of the game but is also a trailblazer for Indigenous men in Rugby. He retired at 26 after steering Australia to win a World Cup and is now very successful in business.

Both men would have been knighted if they were English. Michael is a dual Rugby League/Rugby Union international, and is considered one of the smoothest, most well-balanced runners as well as an incredibly accurate goal-kicker in both codes.

During the tour, I conducted sessions with the playing group and staff on resilience, mental health and social responsibility. However, most players wanted to chat with me one-on-one regarding their lives and their mental health. I loved the camaraderie on that tour: it brought back memories of when I played Rugby Union and made me a little regretful that I hadn't continued with it.

While I now enjoy speaking engagements and believe that my way of portraying my spirituality draws attention when I speak, I must admit I used to ramble a bit. I sometimes exceed my time limit, but I believe I give good value for money. My biggest critic, Pam, pointed out that I tended to beat around the bush instead of going directly to the message. And my observations of the audience's reaction tends to reinforce her opinion.

So these days, my talks are far more measured and to the point.

Some of the forums I've spoken in recently include:

- the World Suicide Prevention Forum in Brisbane
- the Inaugural Australasian Mental Health and Higher Education Conference
- Emotional Fitness Recovery workshops
- Mental Illness Fellowship North Queensland (MIFNQ).

In discussion with Peter Sterling at a mental health awareness function in Townsville in 2015

The latter was with Parramatta and Australia great Peter Sterling in 2015. I also embarked on a MIFNQ road trip with Shayne Webcke who remains the best front-row forward I have seen. Shayne won four premierships with the Broncos and represented Australia 26 times and Queensland 21 times. On the trip, we discussed mental health and offered support to many farmers in the west, and conducted two Rugby League dinners where attendees could hear stories from us both.

The events of the global COVID-19 pandemic coincided with learning about and integrating the news of my Parkinson's diagnosis. My position as Wellbeing and Education Manager for the NRL was put on Jobkeeper: a government subsidy designed to help businesses keep workers employed. However, I decided to take a redundancy six months after Jobkeeper began because I felt that retirement was the better choice for me.

I had no send-off or ceremonies, but then I'm not really one for such occasions anyway.

Of course, my health concerns have also led me to be discerning about the speaking engagements I take on. And in the next chapter, I'll talk about my diagnosis and the way forward.

Australasian Mental Health and Higher Education Conference 2018

CHAPTER 9

Parkinson's Disease – the Storm Builds

You must learn to play with the cards you've been dealt.

The last 20 years have been the toughest of my life in terms of ill-health and the physical breakdown of my body. As is the Australian way, some people would probably call me a 'drama queen' after reading about my various health setbacks.

However, I have the scars – both mentally and physically – to back up my story. It's not that I want sympathy – that's not my way. Nor do I feel bulletproof. I'm just optimistic and I get on with life. I'm a fitness enthusiast, and I'll stay that way for as long as I'm physically able to. As an example, I've just completed a 165 km walk over five days at the time of writing this book.

All shook up

I was diagnosed with Parkinson's disease in January 2020, but the reality is that my right arm had probably started shaking around ten years before. In fact, I haven't been able to use my right hand for writing for quite a while, and I've had to learn to write left-handed. I can no longer hold a beer or a cup of coffee in my right hand now because it shakes uncontrollably. I also have tremors in other parts of my body. Most people don't know that Parkinson's has many internal symptoms as well, and I've experienced some of these such as depression, incontinence and anxiety.

I've read a bit about Parkinson's, but I don't want to find out too much at this stage. I know that something's coming. It's like watching a storm build: I can see the clouds and then I hear the thunder. I know that Parkinson's can't be cured, but that medications can help to control the symptoms.

What I've read tells me that Parkinson's is a degenerative, progressive disorder that affects the nerve cells in deep parts of the brain. It's not a death sentence or even a direct killer, like a stroke or heart attack would be. However, it does bring with it symptoms that are likely to impact my quality of life as it worsens.

The obvious question is why I waited ten years before going to a doctor about it. When I initially felt the tremors, I thought they might have been due to an ulnar nerve operation in my elbow.

> *When the tremors became more frequent and spread to different parts of my body, I knew deep down that something was wrong.*

But – to be honest – by that point, I didn't really want to investigate it.

I suppose I'm like many men who have a misguided aversion to seeking medical care. I've read that the number one reason men avoid the doctor is fear. They worry about a bad diagnosis or a bad outcome. Men also like to see themselves as being strong enough to handle things on their own.

My attitude towards Parkinson's is a result of the bush upbringing that built my resilience. I've seen lots of people working on the land with ailments that city people would want three years' sick leave for. I often tell myself nothing is easy and that getting on with life in the face of adversity is the best medicine.

I also reflect on what so many people around the world must endure. As I'm writing this book, we're in the midst of the COVID-19 pandemic, which has killed millions of people. Another damning statistic is that more than one million children die of starvation each year. There are so many people out there with illnesses worse than Parkinson's. I see a young lad at my gym who's never been out of a wheelchair. He can't move his arms or legs, but he plays wheelchair soccer and manages his life in a truly inspirational way.

What concerns me more than my Parkinson's diagnosis is that MRI brain scans I've had show that I've suffered a stroke at some stage in my life. The neurosurgeon couldn't tell when, and he asked me if I've ever felt imbalanced down one side of my body. I can't specifically recall experiencing something like that.

Again, I'm glad that I'm fit because aerobic exercise is important in helping prevent strokes from recurring. Scans can often discover additional issues. For example, when I had viral meningitis and encephalitis in 2001, my specialist discovered that I'd at some stage gone through dengue fever and glandular fever too.

As I've said, when you've grown up on the land, you just get on with things through sickness, flood, drought and whatever else life throws at you.

It's not just about me

My religious faith has been especially important through all of this. I don't sit for hours and pray to God that I'll be OK, but I do go to Mass a couple of times a week as part of my faith. If God can help me, I know that he will... I don't have to ask for it. The power of faith works wonders for me.

While Parkinson's may cast a dark cloud over my future wellbeing, right now I'm coping well. I'm getting out and meeting people, which I really enjoy as a people person.

Of course, the support of my family will also be important in the years ahead. They've already made incredible sacrifices during my coaching and business careers – in fact, I've put them through massive upheavals. Since Pam and I were married in 1981, we've had 24 different residences!

We've lived in Rockhampton twice, in Mackay twice, in Townsville three times and in Brisbane twice. I recall Yana asking when she was in fifth grade in Townsville, "Dad, can we stay here now? This is the sixth school I've been to."

This made me take stock of what my life was about and what I was doing to my family. No doubt many women would think I'm selfish, and – looking back on my life, as I said in a previous chapter – I'd have to agree with them.

Looking back also on my full-time coaching at the Cowboys, I realise it was an obsession. Since I was away so much, Pam was the glue in our family, looking after our two children's educational and sporting development. Yana was a talented swimmer, winning a Queensland all-comers medley title, while Jarrod excelled at cricket, taking hat tricks on three occasions – twice in representative matches.

In fact, behind every achievement in my life so far has been Pam's support. As we approach 40 years of marriage, I can't recall us ever having a real argument. Yes, of course, we disagreed occasionally, but never about anything major. She now works as a civil drafter, designing roads throughout Australia, and is a fine athlete in her own right, specialising in distance running and swimming.

Through Pam's influence, Jarrod and Yana have grown up to be very balanced, caring people. Yana teaches secondary school Japanese and is head of the department for HPE (Health & Physical Education). She and her husband Matt are parents to two-year-old Vera, who can already count to ten in Japanese.

Meanwhile, Jarrod has run his own construction business for around ten years and is now looking to expand into Queensland's southeast. He's achieved well, given that school was never an interest for him. The four of us are a very close family, even though Yana and he both live in Townsville and Pam and I are on the Sunshine Coast.

We all need a purpose

As I look towards the future, I'm hopeful... I know that the answer is to keep active – if I sit around all day, I just get depressed. Our minds can do funny things because many fears are born of fatigue and loneliness.

I go to the gym five days each week. I find that gripping, pushing and pulling gives me a sense that my body and muscles are doing what they are supposed to, even if the messages my brain sends are sometimes quite slow. This also lets me interact with people, which is good for my state of mind. I don't spend anywhere near the length of time I used to at the gym though.

I also walk every day for an hour or two, always on my own. Earlier in life, I used to run for that length of time. I know that it is a good thing for people with depression to join groups either socially or sports-wise, but I just prefer my own company. I don't enjoy large crowds but love to address large groups. Thankfully, my sisters and brother call regularly.

With all the recent developments in Parkinson's research, hopefully there will be a cure one day... In the meantime, there are many people in this world worse off than I'll ever be.

I do hope to stick around long enough to see Vera, and any other grandchildren I'm lucky enough to end up with, grow up and achieve amazing things in their lives.

In fact, I'm bloody sure I will.

Good times in Japan with Pam in 2017

My family at Yana's big day in 2015: Pam Hurst, Murray Hurst, Yana Hurst-Newton and Jarrod Hurst

Yana, Matt and little Vera at her Christening in 2019

My son, Jarrod Hurst

*With my parents and siblings in 2005:
Jack Hurst, Donella Walton, Hilton Hurst, Noela Hurst,
Peta Fermino, Murray Hurst and Terry McNeil*

December 2020: Yana and Jarrod with Pam's mother, Barbara Exten, aged 98 years

Four generations in December 2020: Barbara Exten, Pam Hurst, Yana Hurst-Newton and Vera Newton

CHAPTER 10
What Now?

When it's all over, what matters is not who you were, but whether you made a difference.

Sport today is about much more than simply what occurs on the field of play. The issue of players' mental health has now become part of the fabric of the game. We need to continue to address it head-on – and not by using empty slogans. Instead, we have to keep pushing the message that everyone should be able to talk about how they're feeling.

I'm proud of the work my team has achieved in this area in recent years. In particular, I'm proud of the programs we implemented to assist players with their mental health and to help destigmatise mental illness.

I've experienced far more good than bad from my time in Rugby League, and all my experiences have enhanced my resilience. Events in my life over the past 20 years have strengthened the gratitude and empathy I originally developed from being raised on the land. Really, I didn't find Rugby

League – it found me. Coaching would certainly have been an interesting career choice if I'd chosen it though. As it was, it became my love and passion.

I was nominated to stand for election as Central Division Chairman on the Queensland Rugby League board of directors. I was reluctant to do this but decided to run because I wanted to make a difference in this role. We already have some top-level administrators in our game. But if we want to continue bringing mentally tough Queensland players through to the top level and continue as the leading sport as well, we need to improve areas of our administration.

For too long in Rugby League, administrators have told our grassroots clubs and their volunteers what will happen. Instead, it needs to be a listening exercise. Administrators must listen to the clubs and hear them when they talk about what the clubs say will work in their areas.

I don't believe in gravy trains. Some people sit on boards for all the trimmings that will come their way. I'm not interested in that. I just want to make decisions that benefit the core business.

Unfortunately, my ideas and philosophies were never implemented.

So, what now?

I concur with comments from Kelvin Giles, who spent over 30 years in Australia's high-performance sport environment, including six years as Performance Director at the Brisbane Broncos. He also held roles as head track and field coach at the

Australian Institute of Sport in Canberra, and as coach of the UK Olympic track and field team.

Kelvin's observations about the machinations of sporting bodies would ring true with many people – including me. He poses several critical – and valid – questions in his article 'Bureaucrats – part sixty-seven' published on his LinkedIn profile:

> I still cannot comprehend how decision-makers in sporting organisations (Boards, Committees, etc) cannot realise when they do not have the competence to make decisions about performance. Is it their egos that get in the way? Is it knowing that they will be found out as being incompetent that sees them continue to surround themselves with like-minded bureaucrats unwilling to be put under any scrutiny? Do they continue endlessly to create a silo that allows them to perpetuate their existence at the expense of those who are the creators of excellence in performance? Whatever the reasons, there are far too many examples of such incompetence.

I've been asked whether the fear of failure has ever been a motivating force for me during my life. Was I a failure as a head coach in the NRL? As I've discussed in earlier chapters, the way I see it is that I never had a proper chance at the top level for political reasons. And that hurt at the time, especially when people I trusted were working against me behind my back.

I certainly don't have a 'poor me' mindset over what

happened at the Cowboys though. I've always wanted to clarify exactly what happened – with honesty and from my own perspective – so that the mistruths told by others don't continue to be taken as gospel.

I've been criticised during my life – and quite often in coaching – for being too soft on people. I've been told that, to succeed, I'd need to be more assertive and even more aggressive. Well, yes, I *am* a softy. But I'd like to think that I've disproven this criticism by way of results. There are always different methods to get someone to give their best. Mine has been through empathy, earning trust and giving clear instruction.

Actually, I believe I'm assertive in my own way. I'm just not loud or aggressive: as the Desiderata says, loud, aggressive people are vexatious to the spirit.

Reflecting on achievements – both personal and as a team – is always satisfying. Success doesn't always mean being the biggest or the best. And in sport, being successful doesn't require winning premierships. Success is about helping people to become better, showing them good direction and working to help them become part of a solid group so they can be proud of their improvement.

This applies throughout business, sport and life.

Career choices are an interesting facet of our lives. How do we know that the choice we made was the correct one? Do we judge it by money, possessions and assets?

For me, success is health, family and the resultant happiness.

I recently asked Pam whether perhaps we should have stayed in the one place, rather than moving house 24 times around Queensland over 40 years. Should I have persevered with the one job rather than accepting different roles working across four or five industries?

She replied that doing the same old thing throughout our lives would have been quite boring. Perhaps because of her upbringing, she genuinely believes that if her husband is happy, she is happy. She also believes that the variety Yana and Jarrod experienced from our moves has made them the resilient people they are today. I wouldn't be surprised: children watch and learn.

As I hope I've managed to communicate in this book, I take great pride in all of my 'former' lives. I've been a kid brought up on the land, a businessman in the airline and construction industries, a father helping to raise a family, and a successful Rugby League coach. And now, I'm looking forward to the next phase of my life, wherever that may lead me.

Of course, I have a big health challenge ahead of me, but I'm up for the fight. For now, I wake every day with the same short-term goal: to be the best I can.

What next?

Knowing so many professional sportspeople and successful businesspeople has made the concept of writing a book very difficult. Sometimes, the idea has even seemed fruitless, given the time, unpleasant memories and cost involved. This memoir isn't meant to match the books that these people have published, nor do I want to compare myself to them. Instead, the purpose of this book is purely to make it clear that our lives can take different, unplanned directions, and that there's always a way forward with regard to accepting change.

My life is far from over, and there are many lessons still for me to learn. You don't need a teacher or instructor to learn – the lessons are simply there for you to notice, take heed of and absorb. The never-ending task is to pay attention.

Nobody ever expected me to follow my father's lead, but I wanted to and his was the only lead I wanted to take. Maturity can come to people at varying ages or stages in their lives. Listening to everyone you meet can educate you and mature you without you even realising it.

I believe this occurred for me naturally as the youngest of five children. I always needed to listen. Respecting and listening to elders and superiors contributed greatly to my maturity. I learnt to listen in order to learn, rather than listen for a break so that I could speak my mind.

Resilience has become an attribute that's commonly spoken of since the mid-2000s, but it's always been around in some form. However, our understanding of it has changed immensely. We used to always be told to 'get up and get on with it'. If we complained about how hard done by we were, someone would question our character. We now know that this isn't real resilience – perhaps at best it's an immediate, short-term fix that can cause long-term problems down the line.

Today, we understand that developing resilience is a process, and that we can acquire it through instruction, presentation and personal commitment. Methods of teaching resilience are now available from several outlets and institutions, and many wellbeing programs include them. I believe that the secret to becoming resilient is to actually *want* to undertake the process. However, we also need to remember that acquiring resilience will take longer for some than others.

I hope some aspect or angle of this book has caught your attention, and perhaps even encouraged you to adopt another outlook in some way.

Through my upbringing on the land, into dashed sporting career hopes, and onwards through my rise to the heights of coaching Rugby League, I've had one guiding principle in life: it's not just about me.

> *My end goal is simple: to be the man I said I'd be.*

There's no shame in being an ordinary man.
There's no shame in being the man I am.

Hear More from Murray

Would you like Murray to speak at your upcoming event? You'll find him to be an engaging and thought-provoking speaker with mny years' experience in the speaking field.

Murray's style has seen him shine in:

- small group interactive events
- large group inspiration
- special event keynotes.

Topics include:

- resilience
- mental health in sport, and of course
- stories from the NRL days!

Contact Murray for bookings at:

E: hurstmurray@yahoo.com
www.murrayhurst.com

www.ingramcontent.com/pod-product-compliance
Lightning Source LLC
Chambersburg PA
CBHW041956080526
44588CB00021B/2766